Shall We Gather at the Potluck

A Heartwarming Look at the Church I Love

Other books by Mike Mennard:
Can't Keep My Soul From Dancing

Shall We Gather at the Potluck

A Heartwarming Look at the Church I Love

Mike Mennard

REVIEW AND HERALD® PUBLISHING ASSOCIATION
HAGERSTOWN, MD 21740

This book was
Edited by Gerald Wheeler
Copyedited by Jocelyn Fay and James Cavil
Designed by Genesis Design
Cover illustration by Ed Parker
Typeset: Bembo 11/14

PRINTED IN U.S.A.

08 07 06 05 04   5 4 3 2 1

R&H Cataloging Service
Mennard, Robert Michael, 1967–
    Shall we gather at the potluck?

    1. Christian life.   I. Title.

            248.4

ISBN 0-8280-1783-2

Contents

The Pastor's New Clothes

ONCE UPON A TIME—as all good fables should begin—there was a pastor.

Though his parish was small and his job only a part-time position, he loved his congregation of about 40. He loved them and served them as if he were their full-time pastor, because he believed that there was no such thing as a *part-time* pastor. Truth be told, in the traditional sense he wasn't even a pastor at all. You see, his congregation was so small, its future so uncertain, that the denomination couldn't possibly rationalize spending the money for a pastoral salary. As a compromise, the local conference asked that the pastor of the large downtown church keep an eye on the brave little group.

But despite its size, its members felt that they needed a shepherd—a pastor—so they pulled together their personal resources and hired someone fresh out of college. They gave him a house to stay in, a petite stipend, and a long list of duties. The young man felt God's calling and took the position, though it paid nearly nothing and offered a heaping helping of stress.

The young pastor had no experience, of course. He had graduated from college with a degree in theology only that spring, but nothing could have primed him for the strain of pastoral life. He was hardly prepared for the fishbowl in which all pastors must swim. Still, he had energy and ideas; he could sing and preach; his wife was friendly and drop-dead gorgeous; and the congregation seemed to like him.

As he became better acquainted with the members of his church, he realized that they were very much like himself. They had questions—many of the same ones that had plagued him for most of his brief life. No, they weren't deeply theological questions, challenging the core of the church's doctrines. Rather, they were thoughts that few had the courage to say out loud. Some of the questions might seem almost trivial at first glance, though if ignored they could fester into an infected sore, like a splinter that remains under the skin. At first glance some of them appeared simple on the surface, yet were multifaceted and complex: Why do some people in the church bug me? Why is church sometimes boring? Do I have to take off my socks for footwashing? Why is there a nominating committee to nominate the nominating committee?

A few individuals had dared to broach the issues, but had felt slapped down—metaphorically, of course. Most simply buried the questions inside themselves and hoped that someone else would ask. Others refused even to voice them because they believed that they were the only ones harboring such seditious thoughts. Everyone else in the church seemed to be content, seemed to like things the way they were, seemed to have no idea that even pastors were thinking those very same questions too.

This last part—the fact that pastors were not immune to such questions—unsettled the young man most. In college he had been "one of the guys," a jokester, the kind of person who gets asked over for pizza and a video. But now that he was a pastor everyone treated him differently. He was a man of God, a voice of Solomonic wisdom, a resolver of ancient quarrels—the kind of individual that you invite to dinner only after scrubbing the house, bathing the kids, and hiding food or anything else that he might consider suspect. Speaking with a mentor who had been in pastoral ministry for nearly 40 years, the young man asked, "Can't they see that I'm just like them?" But the elderly minister replied, "Oh, but you're not. You're their pastor."

For the first time, the youthful pastor glimpsed both sides of the pulpit, both sides of the church board lectern—and a terrible thought gripped him: maybe the experience of many churchgoing Christians is, well, naked. Naked like Hans Christian Andersen's vain emperor.

In one of his most poignant fables, Andersen wrote about an emperor who enjoyed wearing the most expensive, most exquisite articles of clothing in the entire empire. Aware of the emperor's vanity, two conniving tailors persuaded him that they could design and sew the supreme outfit. "We've invented an extraordinary method to weave a cloth so light and fine that it looks invisible," they told him. "As a matter of fact, it is invisible to anyone who is too stupid and incompetent to appreciate its quality."

The emperor commissioned his new outfit from the new material—

no expenses spared. To make a short story shorter, the crooked but clever tailors fitted the emperor with the new outfit, and, of course, the emperor couldn't see it. But rather than reveal that fact and thus admit to being stupid and incompetent, he fawned over the cloth and praised its detail.

The conceited emperor demanded that he be paraded through town. But while everyone could see that the emperor was naked, no one would admit to it. Not wanting to appear stupid and incompetent either, they shouted, "Look at the emperor's new clothes! They're beautiful!"

The pastor wondered if that might not parallel how Christians view much of their experience at church. Such individuals see and think many things about their church, about themselves, and about their Christian culture. And they have questions that they think they should never ask. They're afraid to raise the questions—to express themselves—because they're fearful of appearing stupid and incompetent. No one else seems to struggle with such thoughts, they assume, so they must be alone.

In Hans Christian Andersen's story, however, a little boy at last looked up at the emperor and boldly announced, "The emperor is naked." The boy's father reprimanded the boy and shouted, "Fool! Don't talk nonsense!"

But the deed was done. Someone had had the courage to voice what everyone else was thinking, and the people said, "The boy is right. The emperor is naked!"

And the emperor realized he had been duped.

The young pastor found some humor in this obvious game that he and his congregation seemed to play. *If only people knew they weren't alone in their questions and observations,* he thought to himself. *If only people aired some of those questions, it might lead to a healthy discussion. No doubt there would be a great sense of relief in the discovery that others also struggled with such issues. And maybe the very act of asking the questions out loud might allow everyone to laugh at themselves, which is usually a healthy exercise.*

So the young man devised a plan—more like a sermon illustration. He would walk onto the church platform wearing nothing but shorts and a T-shirt. Then he would explain that he had just purchased a beautiful new suit for pastors, but only those who were truly spiritual could see it. Obviously, the young man didn't think his congregation was so foolish as to believe him—or at least he hoped as much. But the illustration would allow him to talk about the things that everyone sees—just as they could

9

see his near-nakedness—but refuse to talk about. "It's as if the congregation recognizes that I'm naked—well, almost naked—while they praise my taste in clothing," he could explain.

The idea seemed effective, certainly memorable. But as he waited in a back room to walk on to the platform, he looked at himself and laughed. He appeared ridiculous in his shorts and his T-shirt, and he knew it. Then he thought about old Mrs. Reed, who sat faithfully on the fourth row. Her already weak heart might not withstand a second heart attack at the sight of her pastor in a T-shirt and shorts. The young man lost his nerve, and he quickly put his suit back on—the real one that everyone could see.

After the service he felt a little disappointed in himself for abandoning his courage. As he drove home he spoke out loud to himself, as he often did. "Someone needs to address these taboo subjects," he declared, "to ask the questions that we all seem to dwell on but never feel brave enough to deal with in public. Perhaps by shedding light on them, we can laugh at ourselves. Maybe we can discover new paradigms. Or perhaps we might even discover how we've been asking the wrong questions all along. And best of all, we might learn that God is never afraid of our questions, though we sometimes get nervous about His answers."

As the young man rode along, he thought about his invisible suit. "Maybe someone should write a book about the subject."

And though it took him a few years to get around to it, he did.

1

Sometimes Church Is Boring—Is That OK?

BLAME IT ON MY HIGH-FAT, high-carb breakfast if you like. Or maybe it was the inevitable letdown after a concentrated week of midterm exams at Pacific Union College, where I was struggling through my freshman year. Whatever the reason, I knew I was in trouble and would soon be struggling to stay awake.

I had come home for the weekend more than a wee bit tired. Probably I could have slept through the entire weekend, but Mom and Dad had to be at church, and Mom wanted me to see old friends (which really meant she wanted to show off her little baby, the collegian). After a shower and a heaping plate of Mom's pancakes, I climbed into the back seat of Dad's plump station wagon—a smog-gray Chevy with fake wood siding—and we rumbled off to church.

As we pulled into the three-quarters-full church parking lot, I knew the battle would be intense. No, it wasn't going to be a fight with any of my fellow churchgoers. To be honest, I've never been that kind of combatant—and besides, I figured I'd let other church members do the duking it out, if there was any to be done. My fight was going to be with a more potent, more intimidating challenger—sleep.

I do not mean to suggest that our pastor was boring. To the contrary, it was always apparent that he'd sunk hours of preparation into his sermons, searching for the perkiest proof texts and cleverest anecdotes. Sometimes his anecdotes didn't match his proof texts and vice versa, but that was part of his charm. He's the only pastor I know who could take some of the most compelling texts in Scripture, such as John 3:16, and work in a per-

11

tinent tale about his mint-condition 1966 Ford Galaxie 500.

Granted, it was a pretty car with creamy white paint, American steel, and leather seats. I figured he loved the thing an awful lot, because his driveway was usually wet, which could mean only two things: Either his car enjoyed more showers than a bad relief pitcher, or he was obsessively self-conscious about the dirt on his driveway. At the time, I had never considered the latter possibility, but as I write, I wonder if it wasn't a little of both of them.

Anyway, he'd step up to the pulpit, not unlike the way he slipped into the cockpit of his Galaxie 500. Before he'd speak, he'd run his fingers along the outer rim of the pulpit, and I wondered if he imagined it to feel like those hard plastic control panels of his car. Then, as if he'd turned the key and shifted into first gear, he'd begin to preach—slowly.

"I'd like you to open your Bibles to the third chapter of John, verse 16."

This particular morning I was hoping we'd get to third gear before noon, because then I'd have a fighting chance of staying awake.

"Yes, um, the sixteenth verse of chapter 3."

I wondered why he couldn't simply say "Please turn to John 3:16."

"Please turn to John 3:16."

There, he said it. But it took him three tries. Without doubt today's sermon would be a casual drive. Slouching, I tried to merge with the pinkish cloth of the pew. Rubbing my chin's prickly whiskers, I pondered if they'd ever burgeon into a full-blown beard.

"Now, where were we?"

The thought flitted through my mind that I should hold up one of those signs with "John 3:16" plastered on it, like I've seen on televised sporting events.

"Ah, John 3:16. 'For God so loved the world, that he gave . . .' Yes, he gave. He gave us the best he had to give. It's kind of like my Galaxie 500."

I knew he'd figure out a way to work in his car.

"I discovered that car in a junkyard. It actually had mushrooms growing from the lining in the roof. The metal was rusted. The windows were busted. The hood was missing. It seemed to be good for nothing but scrap. It was worthless. And that's the very same condition in which God found me."

Don't ask me how, but it seemed as if he'd skipped second gear and had suddenly hit his stride at third gear, ready to kick into fourth.

"I decided that car would become a living parable. It would allow me to take my love for cars and turn it into a daily reminder of God's love for me. I didn't have any money, but I did have the skills. So I fixed that car up with the best I had to give—my time and my ability. For sure, that car's not perfect, as those of you who may have seen me stuck on 680 will note, but I love it. I love it, not because it's perfect—because it's not—but because I gave a part of me to save it."

I had to hand it to the guy: he had managed to work his car into his sermon and make a memorable point. We were obviously in overdrive now. "Please, Lord, don't let him put it in cruise control," I began to pray.

I'd like to say that I remember the rest of the sermon, but I can't. First, it was some time ago and, more important, I slipped out of consciousness somewhere in the middle. You see, our pastor, a good man, one of the great mentors in my life, preached with the same philosophy that many ministers do.

I don't know where the concept originated, because no theology professor I've ever known has taught it. Most pastors would deny being practitioners of it, but their actions—no, their homiletics—speak louder than their words. (That's a bit redundant, isn't it?) The approach goes like this: If you don't make your point at least six or seven times, you haven't really tried. A corollary might be: The phrases "In conclusion" or "Let me close with this" generally mean the sermon has reached the halfway point.

I should note that our board of elders tried to find a compassionate way to combat this sermon-stretching philosophy. They installed a small red light at the top left corner of the pulpit. This way when the clock struck noon—or when it was painfully clear that a spectacular percentage of parishioners had discovered a new application to Jesus' words "Come to me, all you who are weary . . . , and I will give you rest" (Matt. 11:28), the head elder could press a button and the red light would glow. It would be a lighthouse beacon, a ray of hope for the huddled masses, the tired, the hungry. None but the pastor would see the glow, and, if all went according to plan, he would leap into his closing anecdote and then announce the closing hymn.

In retrospect, the method was neither compassionate nor effective. Rather, it was a failure, and an ugly one at that. Half the church, especially those whose stomach groans announced that potluck was nearing, appreciated the effort. The other half, especially those who believed the Spirit should receive all the time He needed, regarded the light as an abomination. As for myself, I couldn't make up my mind. While I could see the point of giving the Spirit full reign, at the same time I had to struggle with the fact that a lentil loaf was beckoning me and that my gnawing stomach clearly heard its siren call.

No matter what the congregation thought of it, the light never seemed to affect the length of sermons in our church for as long as I remained a member there, which was only another year. (My family moved about an hour and a half north to be closer to where my sisters and I attended college.)

Only recently, upon visiting my old church for the first time in about 10 years, I saw the old pulpit. Wondering if they still used the red light, I tiptoed to the platform, stepped behind the pulpit, and, to the relief of my sense of nostalgia, saw the light still at the top left corner. Looking under the wood panels of the pulpit, however, I could see that someone had mercilessly cut the wires that had ignited the light's glow. No doubt a succeeding pastor.

Bouts with sleep during church are a common struggle, whether Christians want to admit it or not. The red light was an extreme solution to the problem, but it failed, like so many other efforts to try to make church more, well—more interesting.

Now, here's the part of the chapter that may elicit a cringe on the part of some, but it's only because I'm voicing what many—if not most—Christians have thought at least occasionally.

Sometimes church is boring.

OK, I said it. Now that we've cleared the air, let's talk about it.

Sometimes the music is boring. Then again, good music is relative. We had an accordionist who played that thing as if he were wrestling a bear. (And yes, there were some who thought it sounded as if he weren't winning the wrestling match. Personally, I loved it, but I have outrageously eclectic tastes.) Now, I don't mean to suggest that I want every song to be as jumpy as a bunch of frogs on hot asphalt. Nor do I think the funeral home is the model for song selection. (I may be young, but I do know and love those old funeral songs.) I've been to hundreds of churches, many of which have tried to inject excitement with contemporary music. I love contemporary music—I'm a rowdy guitar player, after all. But even in these more progressive churches with their trendy new praise songs, church often gets boring. Sometimes I just crave a good hymn or gospel song. A little variety's not too much to ask, is it? As far as special music goes, all I hope and pray for is a song done well or with sincerity. And before anyone points a finger at me and says, "You can't say that. That's—that's just plain mean!" Just remember that most Christians—maybe all—have thought something similar but are too afraid to admit it.

Sometimes the scripture reading's as long and dry and dull as a badly recited performance of Longfellow's *Song of Hiawatha*. (Well, bad example. I don't think it's possible to have an interesting performance of Longfellow's *Song of Hiawatha*.) It's not that the reading must be Shakespearean or anything. While I'm not expecting the reader to be Charlton Heston in *The Ten Commandments* or *Ben-Hur*—loud, forceful, and overacting—but is it too much to ask that the participant actually read the text beforehand? Or better yet, if we tend to ask people with musical talent to sing or play an instrument (most of the time!), why not insist that Scripture readers have a talent for good delivery? Just a thought.

Sometimes the congregational prayer seems longer than the sermon. We had one elderly man who probably would have prayed for every family in a town of 28,000 by name if he could have remembered them.

Sometimes the most interesting part of church is the children's story. Why is that? Could it be because it's a story? Could that be why Jesus employed stories? And He didn't tell them just to the kids!

Sometimes, when the pastor encourages the congregation to give someone a hug, I feel instant terror. OK, maybe that's just me.

Sometimes the offering call gets presented like a politician's concession speech after losing an election. I thought giving was a blessing, a joy, a privilege. Why not make the offering call a victory speech?

Now, these aren't my thoughts alone. They fill the minds of Christians everywhere, but few will admit it. Some fear that even to *think* about such things is to be critical of the church they love. A number even fear that it is proof that they do not have a strong relationship with God, because, as far as they can tell, everyone around them seems to be enjoying the service just fine.

Here's the truth: Everyone except the pastor finds church boring at times. The only reason the pastor doesn't find it dull is that he or she is working too hard even to stop and think about it. (Contrary to what many believe, pastoring is one of the toughest jobs on the planet, and that's no exaggeration.)

So what do we do?

Do we modernize? traditionalize? compartmentalize?

Do we have a service for the traditional folks, a service for the rowdy folks, a service for the intellectual folks, a service for the shoutin' folks, a service for the whispering folks, a service for the Bible thumpers, a service for the praise-and-worshippers?

We've tried this approach quite a bit lately. I'll let someone with a better finger on the pulse of the church decide whether it has worked, but I'd like to offer an alternative, a new paradigm altogether.

Not long ago at my parents' church, a few members mustered the courage to take this familiar (but hushed) gripe directly to their pastor. One slightly disparaging member went so far as to ask, "Is church boring by necessity or by default?" When I heard that, it genuinely surprised me. Every time I'd visited that congregation, I could feel the Spirit of God working. Although much about the service was highly traditional, much was not. Indeed, I felt their service was many things, but never boring.

The pastor had obviously been around the church block a few times, with more than 30 years of pastoral experience. (Anyone who survives 30-plus years of pastoring deserves an extra star in heaven—maybe a trophy in the shape of a Pepto-Bismol bottle on their heavenly fireplace mantels in their supersized mansions.) That many years of experience can make some pastors cynical, but the years had only made this pastor wiser and more empathetic.

After listening to their gripes—exceptional only in that his congregation had the courage to voice them—he turned the tables on them. "I think you're missing the point about church," he said. "You want a more interesting service, but you're thinking of worship as if you are the audience. Truth is, you are not the audience. God is. The real question ought to be Is church boring to God?"

That got me to thinking—always a dangerous pursuit. What would tax the patience of God? I know what sometimes leaves me exhausted from church, but is God ever bored? Or put more positively, what *excites* God?

Does He have a favorite style of music? a favorite song? a favorite

Bible verse? a favorite offering call? a favorite tone of organ? a preferred order of service?

Does He think that every church session should have a sermon?

In one of his most impassioned psalms, David wrote, "You do not delight in sacrifice, or I would bring it; you do not take pleasure in burnt offerings. The sacrifices of God are a broken spirit; a broken and contrite heart, O God, you will not despise" (Psalm 51:16, 17). David wrote this as a distraught plea, begging God's forgiveness for a truly horrific sin. Of course, we don't offer barbecued animals to God anymore, but I think we can transplant the truth of this psalm to our time. Simply put, God doesn't love our worship rituals. Those rituals, many of which originated from our own need for tradition, have always been for *our* benefit, not His. What God finds absolutely irresistible is a repentant heart, a spirit that wants nothing more than to be right with Him.

If that is true, then David's little prayer, desperate and brief as it is, brought more pleasure to God than the rivers of blood that flowed from the ancient Temple. And that same heart and spirit today bring more joy to God than the most skillful songs, the most persuasive offering calls, the most dramatic scripture readings, the best-prepared sermons.

So does God have a favorite style of church?

Yes. It's a church with worshipers who come to Him with broken and contrite hearts. God never gets bored of that kind of church. That's the kind of church I want to belong to. Or better yet, that's the kind of church I want to *be*.

Why Do I Need to Witness When We Pay the Pastor to Do That?

AS OUR CHURCH'S PASTORS and elders left the stuffy room, they probably thought they'd stumbled onto a mother lode of genius. Their idea may have been just that—genius. Or it may have been the kind of obtuse thinking that frequently takes shape when too many people cram into a room without any windows. My personal theory is that they had consumed all the oxygen in the room and had begun to slip into insanity, and while in this state of mental derangement, they had hammered out what they mistakenly regarded as an inspired concept.

On the surface, their idea seemed well-meaning enough: *Let's visit every former or nonattending member of our church.*

I was about 16 at the time and extremely active in our youth group. Because he was a church elder, my dad had helped to formulate this radical idea, so I tried to be gracious about the whole thing. My first inclination was positive. It seemed like an appropriate, even brilliant little brainchild. Until I learned more.

And rather than have the pastoral staff do the visiting, let's send out the church members. After all, some people don't feel comfortable having a pastor in their home.

Yes, I agreed, and some people don't feel comfortable having the cable guy in their home, but they don't call a plumber to install their HBO. So what's the point?

I tried to comfort myself with the age factor: Being only 16, I could hardly be expected to visit anyone.

We'll have peers visit peers.

Good. Good. But what about the youth? Who was going to contact them?

We'll even have our youth visit the youth.

Suddenly I had a rare moment of speechlessness. It was as if I had received my draft card, and now I contemplated a one-way trek to Canada. Was there such a thing as a conscientious objector in such situations? Maybe I could organize the youth into a rally? paint protest signs? have everyone join hands and sing "Blowin' in the Wind" or something?

After my dad explained how the decision had come about, I asked the same question that probably most Christians have raised: Don't we pay the pastors to do that kind of work? I don't like visiting people and talking about their spiritual lives. That's why I'm not a pastor. And that's why he makes the big bucks. (Boy, was I naive!)

Dad and I talked about the plan, and I tried to be frank about my apprehension. I told him that I'd rather have an ingrown toenail that gets infected and leads to gangrene and the eventual amputation of my big toe than visit people I didn't know. What if they were serial killers? Or what if they were Dallas Cowboys fans? Be real, Dad. How could I have a spiritual exchange with a Dallas Cowboys fan? Did you see what the Cowboys did to the 49ers this year? (I prided myself for my knack for keeping my priorities straight.)

"Well, I don't want to visit people either," he replied.

"What?" I screeched in horror. "But you were in that room! You were a part of the decision! And the pastor said you were all in 'one accord' about this, and I don't think he was making Honda jokes."

"Well, sometimes it's not that easy, Mike."

I didn't have to think about it for long before I understood what he meant. It's a difficult thing to express apprehension when everyone else seems to feel that something is the right thing to do—or, more accurately, no one has the courage to say otherwise. To express reservations would make one appear, well, unspiritual. In such situations 2 Timothy 1:7 gets in the way more than it helps. For some reason, the well-meaning promise that "God did not give us a spirit of timidity [that is, fear]" has kept many Christians from admitting that they are scared. After all, they certainly didn't get that apprehension from God, so it's not OK to have it. It's better to hide it than to admit to having something ungodly churning in one's stomach. (And before anyone declares, "You can't say that!" one has to admit that there is at least some truth to what I've just stated.)

19

"So do you think you were the only one in that room who didn't want to go through with this?" I demanded.

My dad thought about that one. "No, probably nearly everyone felt as I did. I believe most of us are scared." (See! I told you so!) "But the pastor laid the gospel commission on us pretty thick, and who wants to appear anti-witnessing?"

I considered that for a moment before concluding that if I had been in the room I would have done the same thing; I've always had less nerve than my father. There was no escaping it: A few unsuspecting people were about to receive a little visit from me—ready or not.

The church gave me five names to visit. I knew only one of the individuals and decided to start with that one in order to work up my courage for the others. Breathing in through my mouth, out through my nose, to prevent passing out, I called her—her name was Betsy—and told her we had missed seeing her around lately.

Betsy was a grade ahead of me and had attended our local church school for a number of years, but she'd gone to public school now for about three years. At first she had continued to come to our church, but we hadn't seen her much in the past two years. I had always liked her. She was a bit giggly, but still kind of cute and fun to be around. I called her on the phone to ask if I could stop by her house sometime to visit—you know, just to say hi.

The few seconds she did not say anything felt like a decade. I wondered why I felt as if I were asking her out on a date. No, this was even more stressful than arranging a date. Indeed, in that situation I tell myself that the worst-case scenario is that she'll laugh at me, mock me for calling, tell everyone at school that I phoned, and start a schoolwide chant: "Mike got rejected." (But I don't mean to dredge up my dating life.) Maybe she thought I was a stalker, or a psychopath, or another multilevel-marketing representative. Or maybe she assumed that I was a vicious churchgoer who wanted to drag her into the town square to be stoned to death.

"Mike? Mike, are you still there?"

"Sorry; did you say something?"

"Why don't you come by on Tuesday night, if that works for you?"

I couldn't believe it. "Tuesday works great. See ya about 7:00."

Hanging up the phone, I could feel a tightening in my chest. Was I too young to slip into cardiac arrest? After breathing into a bag to prevent hyperventilation, I came to a more terrible realization: That was the easy part! I was committed now. I had to visit her. "Lord, if it is possible, let this cup pass me by," I prayed. "Or better yet, can I have another cup with something easy to swallow in it—an ice-cold raspberry lemonade, perhaps?"

Not surprisingly, God didn't respond to my prayer. Or if He did, He sure didn't give me the answer I wanted to hear.

For the moment I didn't book any more visits. I figured that I'd wait to see if I survived this first encounter before I ventured out further. "Lord," I prayed, "if You'll just get me through this visit without too much humiliation, I'll call the other four people on my list. I promise."

Tuesday arrived, and the only thing I could think about all day was the impending appointment. As I blindly stumbled through my routine of tenth-grade classes my mind was busily preparing for difficult theological questions that Betsy might spring on me. Even in biology class, where we dissected a fetal pig, I could only wonder if my dignity would suffer the same fate as this poor pink creature. At lunch I didn't have the stomach to eat my kidney bean sandwich (one of my favorites), but I'm not sure if that was because I was stressed about that evening or because I couldn't get the nauseating smell of formaldehyde off my hands.

After a miserable supper (because of my nerves, not the food), I drove over to Betsy's house. Actually, I drove with my dad in the car because, though I was 16, I still had only a learner's permit. So as if the visit itself weren't humbling enough, I had to go through with it while my father waited in the car outside.

We pulled up to Betsy's house, and I half-jokingly said, "Keep the car running. This could get ugly." Then I grabbed my small daypack, in which I had stuffed my Bible and a smartly designed flyer advertising the church's weekly "Youth Night." I knocked on the door and prayed hard. Perhaps the amount of praying I had been doing—mostly out of sheer terror—was justification alone for the whole witnessing effort.

Betsy's father answered the door and immediately let me in. Her family was Middle Eastern—Egyptian, I think—and ornate trinkets, the kinds of knickknacks I imagined one might uncover in an archaeological dig, filled the house. Her father was a friendly guy, and he remembered my name, which eased the tension. "Step into the living room, Mike. Betsy told me you were coming." Then I nearly lost my skin when he turned and hollered, "Betsy! Get down here! Mike's here!"

Although I had a prepared speech, when she entered the living room, the words seemed silly. Instead, I decided to wing it. When I opened my mouth to speak, Betsy immediately interrupted me. I remembered that she could be talkative, but I'd forgotten just *how* talkative. Or maybe she was more nervous than I was and talking helped to ease the stress.

"You know, Mike, I've been meaning to check out your youth group. Is that still going on? I hear you guys do fun stuff. Didn't you have a recent backpack trip?" She looked at me and waited for a profound reply.

"Uh, yep." (Were those the only words I could muster?)

"I've never gone backpacking, but I'd probably like it. Except for the whole outdoor thing. Oh, the sleeping on the ground wouldn't be too great, either. And I'm not too big on campfires or tents or hiking. But I do like eating ramen. Don't you eat a lot of ramen when you go backpacking?"

"Uh, yep." (Again, the same annoying words. You can do better, Mike.)

"Anyway, I think I'll start coming to your youth group, if you don't mind. Is that OK if I come, even though I don't come to the church too often?"

"Uh, yep." (There had to be something more profound to say. But what?)

Suddenly she seemed to stop and catch her breath, and then she asked, "What did you come here for, anyway?"

At this point I really could hardly remember. "Uh, I came to invite you to our youth group. We meet every . . ."

"You meet every Thursday night, right?"

"Uh, yep." (For the next visit, if there was one, I'd bring a thesaurus or something so I could come up with some more engaging, more spiritual words than "Uh, yep.")

"OK. Well, I gotta run. Sorry we can't meet for long, but I promised my friends I'd join them for a late-night run to the mall. You know how it is when the mall calls." At that she giggled wildly. It was a bit scary.

"Thanks for letting me drop by," I managed to stammer. "Hope to see you at the youth group."

As I slid into the car I glanced at the digital clock on the dashboard. Nine minutes. The whole thing had lasted nine minutes! And I never said a single spiritual word, not one pious nugget of wisdom. Not only did I not even pull my Bible out of my bag, I'd even forgotten to hand her the invitation to Youth Night.

"That didn't take long," Dad commented. "How'd it go?"

"I don't know," I answered, still a little stunned. "I don't think it went very well."

"Why?" my dad asked as he drove away from Betsy's home.

"I said absolutely nothing—nothing spiritual, anyway. I didn't even pray with her. In fact, I didn't do anything. It was a wasted trip." I replayed the visitation again and again in my mind, searching for some moment I could point to as a spiritual one. Somewhere in our very, very brief chat there must have been a moment where the gospel got preached. But no, I had failed.

That's when I got angry—partly with myself, partly with my father, partly with the church, but *mostly* with our pastors. *There's a reason that pastors—and not I—should do this kind of stuff,* I thought to myself. *They're trained to do it, and I'm not. They're experienced at it, and I'm not. They're good at it, and I'm not. And most important, they're paid to do it, and I'm not.*

Two days after the traumatic visitation, I attended Youth Night, partially to see if Betsy would show up. If she did, then I might consider the visit a success. I'd proudly announce that a seed had been sown that night, and that I was the brave sower. Our youth pastor had planned a special evening of volleyball and videos, hoping we might see some new faces that night. And there were a few. Just not Betsy's.

After that, I refused to call the other four people on my list. My first experience had been such an obvious failure that I thought it would only be compassionate of me to stay as far away from them as possible. As a matter of fact, my witnessing skills were so abysmal that I might inflict permanent spiritual damage on them.

A week or two passed, however, and I began to feel guilty. Of course, in the Christian life guilt is often a four-letter word, a kind of cancer we ask God to amputate from our lives. After all, Paul tells us—in another one of those badly misused texts—that "there is now no condemnation to those who are in Christ Jesus" (Rom. 8:1). Hence some have mistakenly argued that if we feel guilty, we must not be "in Christ Jesus." But this guilt was no cancer, and I knew there was no point asking God to remove it as long as I was shirking my responsibility. No, my shame was more like the Jonah strain, the kind one feels after hopping on a ship for Tarshish when one should be making tracks for Nineveh. One might even call such guilt the Spirit-prodded variety.

Pulling out the small sheet of paper with the four unvisited names on it, I stared at the first name intently: Brian Jenson. Then I prayed, "Give me a few days to work up the courage, God, and I'll call Brian Jenson, whoever Brian Jenson is."

Before the next Youth Night I arrived early to help our youth pastor—Pastor Ron—set up. I'm sure Pastor Ron thought I was an over-achieving goody-goody or an eager beaver by showing up so early to help, but I had ulterior motives. As we set up a large TV screen to watch a movie that night—believe it or not, videos were pretty new and gimmicky at this time—I asked him a few questions straight-out. "Why are we visiting all these people? Isn't that *your* job? Isn't that what we *pay* you to do?"

At first he seemed surprised by the question. "When Jesus commanded us, 'Go, therefore, and make disciples of all the nations,' was that a minister-only request?" he replied. "Did He say, 'Go, therefore, and make sure your pastors are making disciples'?"

I had already considered that possible approach, so I thought I had him. "Obviously not, but let's not forget that Jesus was talking to His disciples, who, you might say, became professional preachers—like you."

Pastor Ron reached for his Bible and started thumbing through the pages. It looked like he was desperately looking for an answer, as if he didn't actually have one, but he did. (He *always* did.) When he landed on a text in 1 Thessalonians, I knew I was in for a mini-sermon.

"Think of it this way, Mike. When Paul traveled from city to city throughout the Roman world, he followed a very basic plan. First, he persuaded a few about Jesus' divinity. Then he helped them form little societies we call 'churches,' and he taught the people how to follow his example so those churches would grow. When the people were able to keep things running without his help, Paul moved on to the next city. In a sense, Paul was always working himself out of a job. A good pastor is trying to do the same thing—trying to work himself out a job."

"Yeah, but . . ."

"No, it gets better," Pastor Ron continued. "Paul had set up a church in Thessalonica, a highly educated and savvy region of the world. The new believers there must have been amazing people, because their numbers grew in large part because of the way they lived their lives. So Paul wrote them a letter to keep the success story going. Apparently, according to him, they had become 'imitators of us and of the Lord; in spite of severe suffering.'"

"OK, but . . ."

"What's more, they had become 'a model to all the believers in Macedonia and Achaia,' and their faith inspired people to become believers throughout the whole region. Their witness was so effective that Paul said he didn't even have to say anything to evangelize the region. The believers had already persuaded their neighbors."

"I understand, but . . ."

"In other words, Paul had worked himself out of a job, and he didn't seem to mind."

I thought for a moment, and then asked nervously, "So what happens if you're successful? Does that mean you'll move on to the next city?"

Pastor Ron smiled but didn't answer.

Members of our youth group filtered in, so I thanked him for the sermon. "Was that a sermon?" he said. "Sorry. Next time I'll collect an offering."

I joined some of my friends and talked about life's nuts and bolts: who was dating whom, what was happening this weekend, why it was so difficult to remove the plastic shrink-wrap from a new cassette. (In retrospect, we lived in such ignorance back then. We had no idea how much harder it would be to remove that annoying plastic once CDs hit the market!)

Pastor Ron encouraged everyone to sit, and as we did I saw two people enter the room. In shock, I sucked in a lungful of air and nearly choked on my own spit. One was Betsy. Still coughing from my near-choking episode, I shouted, "You came! Hey, Betsy, come and join our group!"

She waved to me and walked in, while her friend, a skinny brown-haired guy with freckles on his beefy arms, followed her. I announced to the group, "Everyone, in case you haven't met Betsy, this is Betsy."

I was so glad that everyone welcomed her warmly, as if she were a celebrity, only without the popping camera flashes.

Betsy then said, "I hope you don't mind, but I invited my good friend.

His name is Brian Jenson. I called him up and asked if he wanted to come."

"I told her," Brian interjected, "that all I was looking for was an invitation."

A month later I had completed all my visits, and I couldn't wait to tell Pastor Ron. When I saw him across the church, I ran to him in order to tell him the good news. But when he glanced at me, he seemed sad. "Mike, I wanted you to be one of the first to know that I was offered a job in Maryland, and I think I'm going to take it."

Not knowing what to say, I just gave him a hug and said, "Perhaps you just worked yourself out of a job."

3

Is It Just Me, or Are Some Potluck Entrées Scary?

I HAVE A LOVE-HATE relationship with potlucks. Maybe it's a love-fear relationship, because for the most part I love them, but occasionally I approach them with dread. My reasons may be psychosomatic, but I doubt that I'm not the only one who has ever asked: "Is it me, or are some potluck entrées scary?"

Recently Michelle and I visited a church where we had never sampled its potluck. One can often measure the quality of a congregation by that of its potlucks. I'm not referring to the caliber of the food, because after having assessed hundreds of potlucks at hundreds of churches, I've come to the definitive conclusion that nearly everyone has the same cookbook. When I speak of *quality,* I refer to the aspect of fellowship.

As we entered one church, we were warmly greeted in the lobby with an urgent appeal—not for money, but for our presence at the potluck after the worship service. We immediately felt at home at this church, and because we had no other plans, we accepted the invitation.

Allow me this little aside: Isn't it amazing how far a little kindness goes? I will gladly pay more money to visit a store if I know the service will be friendly, as opposed to the cheaper outlet where I feel like a Giants fan in Dodger Stadium. Sometimes a friendly smile, a warm handshake, a pleasant greeting seem like the rarest and most valuable commodities in the world. Wouldn't if be great if the lobbies and foyers of our churches contained the richest and most consistent supply of kindness? Just a thought.

During the worship service itself, people again implored us to attend the potluck. First, during the "announcement" time a scrawny figure who greatly resembled a scarecrow stood before us and said, "We especially want to invite our visitors to the potluck after the church service."

After appraising the man's scarecrow-like features, my first thought was that I now knew why I hadn't spotted any crows. My second thought, however, was *When was the last time he attended a potluck?*

Later, during the "welcome" portion of the service, a portly man who reminded me of Lou Costello of Abbott and Costello fame again proffered an invitation to us, saying, "Our potluck is especially for our visitors, so please plan to stay after the service."

I leaned over to Michelle and said, "If he could talk Abbott into showing up, the two of them could run through the old 'Who's on First?' routine." Michelle's spiky elbow dug into my ribs, and I winced.

Before the pastor launched into his sermon, he announced, "Just a reminder—there is a potluck after church, so please, please, please do join us."

Wow, I thought. *Three "pleases."* I nearly leaped to my feet, stepped onto the pew, and shouted, "Enough already! We're coming to the potluck!" But that would have frightened at least a few, Michelle most of all. So I restrained myself.

Halfway through the sermon—just about the time I was wondering if I could memorize Tolstoy's *War and Peace* in the amount of time it had taken the pastor to get to the thesis of his argument—a smell wafted into the sanctuary. It was an exhilarating fragrance, a scent that would have driven weaker individuals insane. And it was a smell that can be conjured only by the combination of any known food substance with mushroom soup. Yes, it was the smell of potluck.

I've never been a conspiracy theorist, but my mind grew suspicious. This dear church filled with dear people really *really* wanted us to attend their dear potluck. And now they had resorted to desperate measures, for surely they were pumping heavenly smells into the church sanctuary solely for my benefit. It was a cruel and effective means of enticement. I considered stomping onto the platform, wrenching the lapel mike from the pastor's paisley tie, and shouting, "We told you we were coming to the potluck, but this obvious method of coercion has gone too far!" But I feared that such a radical act might put at risk our invitation to the potluck. What's more, such a terrible reaction (overreaction?) would have ensured a place for me alongside the neighbors' dog that night and, quite frankly, I've never been fond of the neighbors' dog. Hence I restrained myself again.

The sermon ended just before I had completely drowned in saliva. As the people rose from their pews (some adjusting their necks after a prolonged nap), Michelle and I felt immediate affability exuding from the congregation. Complete strangers greeted us as if we were relatives who had come to visit. (If you think about it in the spiritual sense, we kind of were.) Some just said, "Thanks for joining us," which meant more to us than they could know. But most gave us the official church handshake—a vigorous pumping with the right hand and a crushing elbow squeeze with the left—and said, "Please, won't you join us for our potluck?"

At this point I began to wonder if there was something extraordinary about their potluck. Could it possibly live up to the hype? We'd received more invitations than a millionaire at a fund-raiser would have, so the potluck must have had a distinctive quality that set it apart from the other two or three hundred that we'd previously sampled.

A woman led us to a large hall they called the "Friendship Room." It was obvious the room served multiple purposes, because it had basketball hoops, a stage, Pathfinder banners hanging from the wall, and rows of tables for eating. "This must be the multipurpose room," I commented.

She stopped, looked at me, and snapped, "No, it's the *Friendship* Room." Apparently I had struck a nerve. Later I learned that much blood had flowed—figuratively, of course—over the name of that room. But get one thing straight, it was most definitely *not* a "multipurpose room." It was difficult to imagine anyone from this church fighting over the name of a room, but after a whiff of food smacked me upside the head, I didn't care what they labeled the place. Why not call it the "Place-Where-We-Eat-Potluck-and-Play-Basketball-and-Attend-Concerts-and-Hold-Pathfinder-Meetings-and-Refuse-to-Call-It-a-'Multipurpose-Room' Room"? There, I had solved their impasse. It was a catchy name for a room, and it rolled off the tongue rather nicely.

After a well-dressed man thanked the women for making such a fine lunch (and I wondered if there were any men who had contributed to the meal and, if so, how they felt about the host's well-meaning words), the pastor had a brief blessing for the food.

Now, I don't mean to get picky, but has anyone besides me ever wondered about our prayers over food? The words are so often the same:

29

"Thank You for this food, and may it nourish and strengthen our bodies."

The way I see it, food is food. It's going to strengthen and nourish our bodies because, well, that's what food does. Perhaps God gets tired of our asking the obvious. Why not pray for a real miracle? We might demonstrate true faith by praying, "God, we know this food will strengthen and nourish our bodies, and we thank You for that. But we also pray that the food will not make us drowsy and overwhelm us with the irresistible temptation to sleep all afternoon." Now, *that* would be a miracle.

The man continued his prayer: "May we come away from here with renewed energy to advance your kingdom."

Allow me to translate: "We know we're going to leave this place stuffed and lethargic, but at least give us strength to make it to our cars so we can drive home and take a long nap."

"And bless the hands that prepared it."

This is a nice thing to ask God for, but I remember Mom waking up at 5:00 in the morning to prepare two or three dishes for potluck. Somehow I couldn't help believing that she had been cheated. What about her other body parts? Couldn't she have those areas blessed as well? What about the feet that ached from standing on the kitchen linoleum all morning? What about the blister on her forearm from when she pulled her walnut patties out of the oven and accidentally brushed against the grill? I think the prayer should go something like this: "God, we are so blessed by the labor of those who prepared this food. Show us how we can be a blessing to them today."

For many years I worked for a large Christian relief organization. Although I thought I knew what hunger was, I was not prepared for the constant barrage of images—children with softball-sized kneecaps and skin that hugged their protruding bones like Saran Wrap. Every day 24,000 people die from hunger-related diseases, and every night more than 800,000 people go to bed malnourished. Perhaps our blessing before potluck—before every meal, for that matter—ought to be simpler: "Wow, God! We don't deserve Your blessings, but thank You for being so generous."

After prayer, the pastor encouraged the women and children to go first, along with the visitors. This alarmed me. "Women and children first" is usually the cry before a ship sinks. Nonetheless, Michelle and I lined up with the women and children—mostly the children—and I decided to see how many potluck staples I could identify.

Food is a subjective thing, I realize. One individual's gourmet treat is another person's dog chow, so one should understand that my observations and tastes may be mine alone, but bear with me.

As we approached the table, I recognized the fare as if I had stepped up to the potluck table at my home church. It looked like the exact menu I had seen at nearly every church—even the order of entrées was the same. First I searched for the potato chip casserole, and sure enough, there it was. Apparently someone had discovered that if you mix a can of mushroom soup with something, anything—potato chips, lentils, walnuts, rice, and of course gluten—then one has a bona fide potluck surprise. Notwithstanding, there are few surprises left, now that church cooks have tried nearly every combination known to humanity. If I were offering financial advice to the church (and I'm not), I'd recommend buying a large number of shares in Campbell's mushroom soup. It's called putting your money where your mouth is.

Farther down the copiously laden table I entered the gelatin zone. Anytime someone complains about a lack of creativity in the church, I remind him or her of the gelatin zone at potluck. To make a good gelatin one needs only to find an animal-free mix, one that avoids the use of pigs' feet or any other joint or tendon from an animal's body. (How do pigs' feet become a jiggly dish people so enjoy swishing around in their mouths? Come to think of it, I don't want to know.) The actual creativity, however, lies not in the making of the gelatin, but in the ingredients added to it.

Scanning this particular array I saw some of the usual suspects: carrot shavings mixed into orange-flavored gelatin, walnuts and whipped cream blended with lime-flavored gelatin, slices of peaches or nectarines in red (I think it was cherry-flavored) gelatin. At this particular potluck I gazed in horror to find broccoli and cauliflower mixed into green gelatin molded into the shape of a maple tree (or was it an atomic bomb blast?). While it's obvious that somebody appreciates such creativity (otherwise we wouldn't find such a plethora of gelatin options), I'm not sure God intended vegetables, nuts, and gelatin to go together. Fruit, maybe, but certainly not carrot shavings. To be honest, the practice of experimenting with gelatin seems unnatural, like genetic engineering, a bit too much like Dr. Frankenstein piecing together his monster. Sometimes I simply crave just a scoop of flavored vegetarian gelatin—a dull recipe with no carrot shavings or broccoli—and a dab of whipped cream. Now, that's all the creativity I need.

At nearly all potlucks the hosts place the French bread and rolls at the end of the table. The theory is that one can simply lay the bread on top of one's heaping plate, like hoisting a flag at the top of Everest after reaching the summit. But it's clear that the bread serves a more fundamental purpose.

First, I can spot the good French bread a mile away (or at least before I've even picked up my plastic fork and spoon). Usually it comes wrapped in aluminum foil so the butter can saturate every slice thoroughly. The bread is not done right unless it comes out of the foil dripping. It should be a bit soggy, like a wet newspaper. And the expert potlucker keeps the bread away from the gelatin because the latter turns the bread green or red or blue—depending on the gelatin's shade—and who wants to eat blue bread? Absolutely no one—that is, until the end of the meal. You see, after Everest has been reduced to Happy Valley on one's plate, it is the work of the French bread to soak up the valley's obvious flooding problem. The skilled potlucker dips his or her bread into the nondescript fluid—a mixture of juices from the mushroom soup, the salad dressing, the gluten, and the gelatin—and drains Happy Valley of its overflowing streams.

Dessert always made the meal more complicated. I considered myself an experienced potlucker, but it was still difficult to choose between the obvious homemade desserts and the store-bought varieties. If the homemade item was good, it was usually *really* good. But if it was bad, it could out-shame the infamy of gelatin with carrot shavings. A store-bought pie could rarely top a good homemade one, but it was at least a known entity. So what should one do to solve this dilemma of Solomonic proportions? Thousands of good potluckers have discovered the answer: take multiple desserts! But it's always important to make it appear as if one is gathering desserts for more than one person. Unfortunately, I usually sit down to eat my brownie, apple pie, and strawberry cheesecake, only to have Michelle ask, "So what did you bring for me?"

Not to stray too far off the subject, but Murphy's Law of Potlucks states that if one selects an entrée he or she dislikes, its maker will invariably sit across the table and ask, "So what do you think of my dish?" I've found this to be true again and again. Even at this particular potluck I saw a bowl of what looked like apple sauce. Considering the complexities of all the dishes, it soothed me to think that someone had brought an item as basic as apple sauce. I heaped two large servings onto my paper plate. When I sat to eat, I met the dish's maker, a sweet woman with the hint of a Southern accent. She sat across the table from me and explained how she had used an old recipe to make this family favorite. As I shoveled a large spoonful into my mouth she said, "It's been a long time since I made mashed turnips."

I'm not sure if it was the dish's flavor—exactly how I imagine wet particle board to taste—or if it was because I expected it to taste sweet like, well, apples, but I could hardly move my mouth. I pushed the substance into the pockets of my cheeks to keep my tongue from torture. At last I managed to move my lower jaw, though a small tear welled up in the outer corners of my eyes. Miraculously, I swallowed, and she asked, "So what do you think?"

I stared at the turnips in amazement and horror. Then I said, grateful for my high school drama classes, "I don't think I've ever tasted anything quite like it."

She smiled and seemed delighted. "I'll get your wife the recipe," she bubbled.

Once stuffed with food, I leaned back on my chair and savored the friendly people in the "Friendship Room." Nothing about this potluck was extraordinary, in spite of the hype throughout the worship service. Nothing, that is, except for the people.

At every table people talked with people. Not in a gossiping hush, but happily and loudly about what their kids were doing at school, about troubles at work, about the sermon, and about how important the church family had become to them. They questioned me about my career, and they didn't seem too unsettled or overly fawning when I told them I made music and worked for a public relations office as a writer. They asked Michelle and me how we met, how we got engaged, how much longer we would wait before we had kids. Best of all, they actually listened when we answered their questions.

Suddenly my status as an expert potlucker seemed in jeopardy. I thought I knew what potluck was really about—mushroom soup and after-church gossip. But clearly I was mistaken. Perhaps this friendly and appealing church potluck offered an updated glimpse at what the early church had been like.

In Acts 2:46, 47 Luke tells us that the early Christians met every day in the Temple courts. "They broke bread [imagine, instead, healthy servings of potato chip casserole] in their homes and ate together with glad and sincere hearts, praising God and enjoying the favor of all the people." Seeing how much fun and fellowship they were having, it's not surprising that Luke adds, "And the Lord added to their number daily those who were being saved."

Potluck is more than mushroom soup. It's about meeting with other Christians. About being "glad and sincere" and "enjoying the favor of all the people." And the early church proved that meals can be a great witnessing tool, as well. Who would have thought that gelatin with carrot shavings could be spiritual?

When Michelle and I drove away from the Friendship Room, we looked at each other in amazement. "Now, *that* was a potluck," she exclaimed.

"Even the mushroom soup casseroles tasted better," I agreed.

Michelle wrinkled her nose and said, "Now, don't you start piling on the food."

I rubbed my belly and said, "It's too late. I already did."

Then we both laughed, still enjoying the favor of all the people.

4

Does the Family With the Cranky Baby Have to Sit by Me?

I'VE BEEN EATING MY words a lot lately. It's part of getting older. All the pugnacious things I said as a cocky youth have now begun to come back to haunt me. For example, when I was young—young enough to know it all—I said I'd never allow my waist to grow as big around as the length of my inseam. My inseam is 30 inches, and my waist is, shall we say, a tad bit bigger than that! Therefore, I've put those words where they belong—in my mouth so I can swallow them.

It's inevitable, perhaps, that the foolish things we say when young will eventually—no matter how long it takes—boomerang back to bite us. The most obvious example in my life involves children in church.

As a young, childless, and fussy churchgoer, I constantly found myself annoyed by the sounds of children in church. The whimpers, the chatter, the giggles, the paper-rustling—it all bugged me. I believed that if I was going to invest the time to attend church, the least I deserved was a quiet, adult-centered environment conducive to worship. Perhaps someone could post a sign over the door of the sanctuary: "No Kids Allowed!" Or maybe a proper man in a black suit with a towel over his arm could greet people at the door of the church and ask, "Would you prefer kids or nonkids today?" Then I could say, "I'd prefer the nonkids section, thank you."

You see, there are some unwritten rules—unwritten, that is, until now—about children in church. As a near lifelong churchgoer, I have had years to study the relationship between children and church, which is how I unearthed those rules. Even more, I feel it's my duty to share them:

First, something about the construction of pews makes them irresistible for children to crawl under. I blame the inventor of the pew, personally. He or she should have foreseen that a large, benchlike seat with at least a foot-and-a-half headroom from the floor would beg for crawling. What's more, the activity inevitably takes place during pivotal moments, such as prayer, offering, or when I'm trying to find a seat but not looking down at the floor.

Second, if the attention span of a human being is one minute for every year of a person's life, then a child of 3 has an attention span of three minutes at best. Should anyone then be surprised that an hour's worth of church is an enormous challenge for even the quietest of children? (As I write this, I'm 35, which may explain why 45-minute sermons can be a challenge. Unfortunately, people would probably look at me strangely if I brought a coloring book to help pass the time.)

Third, it is inevitable that a baby or little child will cry during a baby dedication. I call it the Santa Claus syndrome. After all, who wouldn't howl if a loud man in a suit picked them up?

And last, men are not as capable as women at multitasking, which means it is nearly impossible for a man to keep the kids quiet and retain anything from the sermon.

That said, enter the Heltons, a young family who attended our church in my late teens. In some ways the Heltons were an ideal family. Both the father and the mother looked as if they could have been models. Neither of them worked out or exercised much, but they appeared as if they did, which may have contributed to my distrust of them. No one, I reasoned, should be allowed to look that good without having to work for it. Even their two sons—one was 12, the other 9—might have easily appeared on a cereal box.

I knew the father only as Mr. Helton, and he worked for the government doing something mysterious. I asked him once what he did for the government, and he laughingly said he could tell me, but then he'd have to shoot me. I was impressed. Mrs. Helton, on the other hand, did something far less mysterious and infinitely more difficult: she took care of foster babies. One would think that having two children of their own would have been enough to keep them busy, but Mr. and Mrs. Helton felt a calling to take care of less-fortunate babies. And not just *any* less-fortunate babies— they primarily accepted "drug babies." (Pregnant women who experiment with cocaine, crack, pot, alcohol, or any other drug often don't realize that their children ultimately bear the consequences of their habits.)

Sometimes the infants appeared normal, but other times their faces were flat like a scary doll or twisted like a horror picture. It was difficult to look at them. One thing that was consistent about all the babies, however, was their irritability. At least they all *seemed* crankier than usual to me. Maybe it was only because Mrs. Helton insisted on bringing her infants into the sanctuary. I wanted to point out to her that our church had a mothers' room, not that I knew what went on in there, but she insisted on her entire family sitting together in church.

If the baby became too loud, she'd first try to rock the child. If that failed to bring comfort and quiet, she would carry the infant into the foyer. I remember feeling such a sense of relief when she'd walk out. "If I ever have children (and that's a big *if*), they will be quiet in church," I vowed.

Though I was brazen enough to *think* such mean thoughts about children in church, I was certainly not so ill-mannered as to *voice* them. That would be, well, ungentlemanly. Even unspiritual. I decided that the best way to combat the Heltons' need to disrupt the sacred air of my church experience was to sit as far away from them as possible.

My plan seemed fool-proof. Our church had large windows separating the foyer from the sanctuary, and one could easily stand in the foyer and watch the members locate their designated seats. Of course the church did not officially assign seats, but one would never know that after a few visits. Every family had claimed a specific pew, and every individual had staked out a small plot of pew for himself or herself. When visitors arrived early and randomly chose a pew, they could hardly know the trauma they had inflicted on a family who discovered its cherished pew no longer vacant. Obviously no one would be so boorish as to make them move: "Pardon me, but we have spent many years shaping that pew to fit our rumps, and you are spoiling the perfect fit by sitting in it." I'm sure the thought, however, had passed through the minds of more than a few members.

The Heltons were an exception to the designated seating concept, however. Either they intentionally rebelled against the seating arrangement, or they were oblivious to it, because every week they occupied a different pew. This disturbed many in the church, which may explain why they acquired a label as deliberate troublemakers. Their habit of migrating throughout the sanctuary was troublesome to me, as well. How was I to know where to sit if they refused to find a permanent seat?

I decided to hang out in the back and wait for them to sit, then I'd casually find a seat far from them and no one would grasp my intentions. Unfortunately, on this particular day the Heltons had yet to show. The long announcement period was over, and we'd already reached the scripture reading. Soon we would be praying, which meant I needed to find a place as soon as possible.

By now I reasoned that the Heltons must have had other plans. Maybe they'd slept in. Perhaps they were on their way to Grandma's. Or could they have decided it was time to give me a worship experience free of squeals or coos or gah-gahs? Expelling a breath of relief, I took a position toward the back of the church and prepared to enjoy a quiet, thoughtful, child-free church service.

Moments later a sound startled me. It came as we were kneeling for prayer, and one of our dear elders was only a third of the way through his lengthy prayer list. The sound penetrated my backbone like a needle. Though I kept my eyes shut, I didn't need to look behind me to know who waited in the foyer—the Heltons. And I didn't have to see the baby to realize that she had come for the purpose of vexing me.

After the prayer ended, the organist played two chords, which drew an instinctual "Aaaaaaah . . . mennnnnnn" from the congregation. I slid into my seat and glanced back to see the Heltons, appearing more frazzled than usual, especially Mrs. Helton. As a family they quietly opened the door into the sanctuary and, to my horror, sat next to me. When Mrs. Helton smiled at me, I managed to smile back. Mr. Helton leaned over and patted me on the shoulder as if to say, "And you thought you were going to have a quiet church service."

The Heltons were taking care of an especially challenging baby at the time. The child's mother had used drugs throughout the pregnancy, and the infant—a cute little Gerber baby girl—never seemed to sit still. Surprisingly, though, she had become noticeably quiet as the family sat down. She was calm. Really calm. Too calm. I kept looking across the pew to make sure everything was OK.

Just before the sermon began, Mrs. Helton leaned toward me and asked, "Would you mind if I changed her diaper right here?"

Yes, yes, I did mind. A church pew was no place for such exposure. I felt sure that the experience would warp the child, making her forever terrified to walk into a church for fear of losing her pants. When she turned 50, she might not remember why she felt such anxiety, but it would be there nonetheless. Absolutely, I did mind.

"Of course I don't mind." I couldn't believe I had just said that.

Mrs. Helton reached in her bag for a diaper then turned to me and said, "I think it's a wet one."

I don't know if Mrs. Helton was suffering from a cold or if she had no sense of smell, but I didn't need to look to know it wasn't a wet one.

By now I considered moving to another pew, but that would be too obvious, maybe even hurtful. Doing my best to focus on the pastor's anecdotes, I tried to ignore baby noises or baby smells. It was a lost cause—the scent was too strong.

Just then Mrs. Helton looked at me and said, "Would you like to hold her?"

I didn't know how to respond, but she didn't give me a chance to. She shoved the small baby into my arms like a quarterback ramming a football into the running back's belly. To be honest, I'd never looked at the baby's eyes before—they were beautiful. She gazed up at me as if I were a view of Mount Everest. I thought I saw her smile, but it was probably just gas. Then she closed her eyes and fell asleep in my arms. She was so light, I could have held her all day without ever getting tired.

I confess that I heard nothing for the rest of the service. All I could do was stare at that little girl and think, *God, how can anyone look at the face of a baby and not believe in a higher being?*

After church I remained in my seat, afraid to move lest I wake the baby. At last Mrs. Helton said, "I'd better come and set you free, huh."

"Too late," I said. "I've already been set free—in more than one way."

Later that day I told my friends how exciting it was to hold the Helton's new baby. Everyone looked at me in shock. "You! You held a baby? And you enjoyed it?"

Trying to sound spiritual, I defended myself with Scripture. "Yeah, don't you remember how Jesus said, 'Let the little children come to me . . . for the kingdom of heaven belongs to such as these'?" (I remembered that verse—Matthew 19:14, incidentally—from my grade school days. At last, a memory verse had come in handy!)

One of my more smart-alecky friends said, "I seem to recall Jesus using the word 'suffer' when He talked about the children."

"Very funny, my little King James scholar." (I had to admit, the King James Version did say something like "Suffer the children to come unto me," but not "suffer" in the way I had been interpreting it for so many years in church. In the time of King James the word meant "to permit" or "to allow.")

Then I added, "If the kingdom of heaven belongs to the little children, I'd better get to know a few and figure out what they've got that I don't." I said that with a smile, and we all knew that I was both kidding and quite serious.

The next week I came to church and sat in the very same seat—toward the back where I had the week before. The Heltons, however, sat toward the front on the opposite side. While this may sound like an all-too-good fairy tale ending, I was disappointed to be so far from the family. To relieve my disappointment, I listened intently to the sounds throughout the room. I could hear occasional coughing, throat-clearing, and paper-rustling.

And I heard kids!

They were everywhere, giggling, crying, and wiggling in splendid surround sound. Granted, they weren't paying attention to the sermon, nor were they listening to their parents' repeated shushes, but they were there. They were proof that the church was alive. And I thought about what Jesus had said about the kingdom of heaven belonging to them. I realized, in a rare moment of clarity, that only a child could appreciate the kingdom of heaven, because the rest of us dull, orderly, cautious adults are too busy trying to stand on our own two feet to ever let God carry us.

Not too long ago my wife and I had our first baby, and we named him Ramsey. He was the cutest, most adorable baby in the planet's history, although I may be just a tad biased. (He was also—and still is—the smartest, but that might reflect my bias as well.)

At first it was easy to take Ramsey to church, because he'd sleep through the entire service. That way he didn't make enough noise to wake the sleeping adults (and I mean that in both the literal and spiritual sense). But as he grew older he became wigglier and louder. Like Mrs. Helton, Michelle preferred to hold him in the main sanctuary (except for feeding times, when she'd slip into the mothers' room).

One day we arrived at church and sat toward the back as we often did, so we could easily escape if Ramsey got too restless. Every bitter thought I had ever entertained about how children should be neither seen nor heard at church had come back to smack me in the face—like spitting into the wind. This particular day, however, Ramsey was ornerier than usual (and I felt guiltier than ever for being such a grump in the past). We think he was constipated, but I doubt he'll appreciate my saying that when he reads this as a grown man.

Sitting next to us, a young woman seemed annoyed. If I had to guess, I'd say she was in her mid-20s, and she was dressed in a stiff gray suit like a bank executive. She never looked directly at us or at Ramsey, but from her sideways glances and wrinkled upper lip I knew she was perturbed. No doubt she wanted to move to another pew, but feared hurting our feelings. I could relate to how she felt.

I probably should have asked Michelle's permission, but I just had a sense about what I should do. Before the woman could protest, I gently set Ramsey in her arms. At first she seemed shaken. Then the wrinkles on her forehead that looked like a dead tree disappeared and a smile wrapped around her face. I was thrilled by her response. And Ramsey, to my complete surprise (and relief), quieted down. He looked up at her as if she were a view of Mount Everest. His eyelids fluttered, and he fell asleep. I wanted to say to the woman, "I don't know if you've heard, but the kingdom of heaven belongs to children." Then I thought better of it. Besides, I think she was getting the point.

Of course, having a screaming little wild man running through the house—and I mean that in a good way—can make a young dad reflective. What is it about children that appeals to God? What would lead Jesus to say that "the kingdom of heaven belongs to such as these"?

Remember that when Jesus said those words, He was scolding His disciples (a frequent occurrence in the Gospels). Apparently they didn't like the sound of kids in church. They wanted them kept far away so the grown-ups could have their quiet, child-free time with Jesus. And they especially didn't want them to do anything disruptive, such as leaping into Jesus' lap.

So how did Jesus respond? He said, "Bring them to Me! They trust

Me. They need Me. And though they may not understand your conventions, your rules, your traditions, and your worship preferences, these children want desperately to be close to Me. And I hope you're not too grown-up yet to think that's silly or annoying."

5

Do I Have to Take Off My Socks
for the Foot-washing Service?

I'M OBSESSIVELY MODEST WHEN it comes to clothing. For example, I've never liked swimming in public pools, because I don't like stripping down to almost nothing in public. If I had a body more like Arnold Schwarzenegger and less like the Sta-Puff Marshmallow Man, I might be more enthusiastic about stepping onto a diving board bare-chested. But then again, this may be my own personal peculiarity.

My sense of bodily reserve—a euphemism for fear of showing too much skin—extends all the way to my feet. I don't like to expose them to the world. Even in the confines of my own home I like to wear a pair of thick socks. Unwilling to admit to my strange quirk, I have often told people that as long as my feet are warm, then invariably the rest of my body is warm—which is in no way a lie! Of course, when I make that excuse on a blistering August afternoon, people look at me suspiciously, as if I'm hiding something under that thick fabric.

In our 14-plus years of marriage my wife has bought me four pairs of sandals with the zealous hope that I may bond with a pair. It's a religious endeavor on her part, as she tries to convert me into a toe-baring Bohemian. But she has yet to grasp that the problem is, in fact, my toes.

I have hideous toes. My toes would nauseate the most indifferent podiatrist, no matter how callous (no pun intended) they might be. The problem is that after decades of keeping my feet under wraps, I have made my toes a friendly habitat for fungus. To thank me for providing such a protective environment, the fungus has mangled my yellowed, crusty toe-nails into something fit for a late-night B-movie monster flick. I hope no one is eating while reading this, but it seems important that one fully grasps the disgusting condition of my feet.

It's not that I haven't tried medications. I've used powders, creams, and liquids. Unfortunately, the instructions on most medications require that the feet remain exposed to the air long enough for the remedy to dry. A friend recommended that I soak my feet in garlic, and I smelled like a creamy pasta sauce for nearly a week. Another friend—or at least I think she's one—lent me some sandpaper and encouraged me to remove the fungus with swift brushing movements. As a result, I hobbled in pain for a few days, yet the fungus did not go away.

In the end it just seemed better to keep my repulsive feet hidden beneath the comfort of my thick socks.

The downside to my condition is that I belong to a denomination that periodically—usually four times a year—conducts a foot-washing service. We call it the "ordinance of humility," but I think of it as the "ordinance of absolute humiliation."

In so many ways it's a beautiful ritual that reenacts the actions of Christ in the upper room. Jesus demonstrated great humility by assuming the role of a slave in order to demonstrate genuine service. He took a towel and a basin of water and washed the dirty feet of His disciples, despite their obvious protests. Though any organized attempt to reenact such an event will lose the power of spontaneity, it still retains much of the symbolism. There is just something beautiful about Christians serving Christians—even in a manner that is humbling, which is much of the point.

However, I don't think the disciples had as abhorrently ugly toes as I have. While few "beautiful" feet exist in the world, there are few as ugly as mine. So while most Christians can go through the motions of foot-washing with confidence, I cannot.

My foot-washing phobia grew so bad that often when I arrived at church having forgotten that a foot-washing service had been planned, I inconspicuously slipped out and went home. It demeans me to admit this, no doubt, but more often than not I simply found reasons to be anywhere but at church on those dreaded foot-washing days. (And the obvious decrease in attendance on those days indicates that I'm hardly the only one to have done that.)

In this sense I was—and am—very much like Peter when Jesus knelt

44

in front of him to wash his feet. Horrified, the disciple exclaimed, "You shall never wash my feet" (John 13:8).

But Jesus answered, "Unless I wash you, you have no part with me" (verse 8).

Peter's repugnance had nothing to do with his ugly feet. I'm sure his feet were obscenely ugly, having traveled throughout his life in sandals rather than on Michelins, but back then everyone's feet were ugly. No, Peter's aversion to having his feet washed had more to do with Jesus— whom Peter had already identified as the Messiah—suddenly putting Himself in the unbecoming pose of a slave. And such an act was just that— slave's work, not divine or even royal duty.

Jesus's response to Peter was part rebuke and part appeal—"Unless I wash you, you have no part with me"—and it affected the disciple just as it has me. Peter answered impulsively but honestly, "Not just my feet, but by hands and my head as well" (verse 9). Feeling the same desire to be washed completely clean, I longed to repeat Peter's words—only, I wanted to add the caveat: "But God, may I please keep my socks on?"

I tried to explain my nearly neurotic aversion to foot-washing to my wife, Michelle, but she didn't understand. "I have ugly feet too," she replied, "and it doesn't bother me so much."

She was, it seemed, a stronger person than I was, and I simply needed to suck in my pride—it is, after all, the "ordinance of *humility*"—and go through with it. In addition, my denomination as well as many others recognize it as a mini-baptism. Jesus said, "A person who has had a bath needs only to wash his feet" (verse 10). It seems an appropriate metaphor. While baptism may be like a spiritual soak in the tub (a soak that lasts forever), it's good, once in a while (and it even feels good), to soak one's feet in God's amazing grace now and then. It would be the perfect ritual if it just weren't so unnerving to people like me.

Our congregation, I think, got tired of seeing attendance numbers dwindle on foot-washing days, so they experimented with a new approach. For decades the ritual had been the same, with the men migrating to one room and the women to another. Each room would be equipped with the necessary tools—basins, towels, neatly arranged chairs. But to shake things up a bit, our church decided to designate a third room for families. While a family foot-washing room is common practice today, at the time it seemed imaginatively radical.

"Look, Mike," Michelle said, "now we can attend the foot-washing service and wash each other's feet. And you don't have to worry about what I think about your ugly feet because I've already seen them." (Michelle is such a to-the-point kinda woman, which is one of the many reasons I love her.)

"OK," I said, really meaning it. For the first time, I could enjoy the ritual with all its symbolism and power and not get discomfited by my feet.

After a brief homily, the pastor encouraged the congregation to find one of the three rooms. I nervously grabbed Michelle's arm just to make sure she didn't run away and force me into where the men bared their toes. But she wasn't going anywhere—except to the family foot-washing room.

When we entered, the basins and towels were neatly arranged as always. "I'll wash your feet first so you can get it over with and relax," my wife said quietly. I appreciated her forethought.

While she went to the corner of the room to fill her basin with warm water, I apprehensively removed my shoes, then my socks. There they were—my toes, in all their fungal splendor! Michelle acted as if they were normal feet as she gently ladled warm water over them with her hands. Then she dried them with the small white towel. As quickly as I could, I put my socks back on and felt instant relief.

"I'll go get some fresh water while you take off your shoes," I told her. She agreed, and I emptied the water from the basin, which had a few black flecks of lint from my socks floating on the top. After filling the basin with fresh water, I returned to where Michelle was sitting and knelt in front of her feet. But I couldn't help staring at them. Then I looked up at her. "Well, aren't you going to take your socks off?"

Michelle looked at me in horror. She was still wearing her panty hose, and having never washed a woman's feet, I was surprised to see the nylon still shrouding her toes.

In a surprised but hushed voice, she said, "Mike, don't you know that women don't take off their panty hose for foot-washing?"

"They don't? Why not?"

"Because it would be, well, you know, awkward."

I washed her feet, but I actually felt as if I were washing her socks. After the ritual we prayed, and I said, "No wonder you don't seem to mind foot-washing. You don't have to take off your socks!"

It was an enormous revelation to me—one that most people probably were aware of while I lived in happy ignorance. I guess I could see the point—removing a pair of panty hose is quite a bit more of an ordeal than pulling off one's socks. After I had grasped the logic of it, it made sense. I wondered if panty hose might one day become the trend for men, as well, and then they could simply keep them on throughout the service. Then again, that's probably not a good idea.

Not too long ago a friend asked me to play the guitar for a small gathering of students at Pacific Union College in California. He wanted me to sing praise songs and help to create an "atmosphere of worship." I was thrilled to accept the invitation. However, he didn't think to mention that the "atmosphere of worship" would lead into a foot-washing service. Otherwise I might have found a reason—*any* reason—to regretfully decline the invitation.

We sang a variety of songs, from the old hymns to the latest praise choruses. I played guitar and sang along with one college student at a keyboard and another with a djembe, a congalike percussion instrument.

After the singing, my friend who had organized the event announced that there would be a foot-washing service, and it's fortunate that I'm very good at hiding my terror. I hardly knew anyone at this event, and Michelle wasn't with me. That meant I would have to wash the feet of a stranger, which was not as traumatic as having that same person wash mine.

People immediately found partners, and I waited passively to see if anyone would choose me. And someone did. He looked as if he was about 21, and I smiled and agreed to wash his feet. He appeared as nervous about the whole thing as I felt. When he picked out a chair in the farthest corner where no one could see us, I was relieved by his choice.

"Why don't I wash your feet first?" he suggested.

Good, I thought. *Let's get the hard part out of the way. If he doesn't run away in horror, then I'm sure it will be painless to wash his feet.*

My feet did not seem at all to repulse him. The student was quiet, but not everyone has to be a chatterer. After drying my feet with the traditional white towel, he went to get fresh water and a clean towel while I put on my shoes. When he returned, I took the basin and the clean towel from him while he sat down and removed his shoes. However, when he removed his socks I nearly—but fortunately didn't—let out a gasp. He was missing nearly all of his toes on both feet, including his two big toes. The toes he did have looked undeveloped, like tiny turtle heads just coming out of their shells.

Probably knowing that I desperately wanted to ask him how he had lost his toes, he smiled. "For some reason I was born with funny-looking feet," he said simply.

Don't ask me why, but I blurted out, "Do your feet keep you from doing anything?"

"Nope. They've never kept me from doing anything I wanted to do—except wear sandals without socks. I figure that's a bit more than most can handle."

I wanted to reply, "I know what you mean," but that would have revealed just how shallow I was. Instead, like a corny cheese ball, I said, "Well, you certainly have decreased the odds of stubbing your toe."

As soon as I said it I wanted to kick myself. Surely I had reached a new low. Because of my own personal discomfort, I had resorted to making jokes at his expense. But he laughed and laughed. Finally, after regaining his composure, he said, "Like I haven't heard that one before." Then we both laughed.

After the foot-washing service we all came together and enjoyed another beautiful ritual—Communion. But after we celebrated Christ's death with the bread and the cup, a student got up to speak. He wasn't particularly dynamic, and I don't think he had any pastoral aspirations. But he did have a pastor's heart.

He talked about the foot-washing and asked if it made anyone feel uncomfortable. To my complete astonishment, nearly every hand went up. "Good," the student responded. "It should make you feel uncomfortable. If Jesus had asked us to wash our own feet, I dare say the whole thing would be easier to swallow." I had to agree.

Then he said, and here I'm paraphrasing, "The very thing that makes you feel uncomfortable during foot-washing is the very thing that separates Christianity from all other religions. It's a thing called 'trust.' It takes a lot to trust God to forgive us, when we'd rather work to earn that forgiveness. It takes a lot to trust God to cleanse us, when we'd rather work to clean ourselves. And it takes a lot to accept the help of another Christian, because he or she may discover that you have ugly, dirty feet. But you know what? We all have ugly, dirty feet, and it takes an enormous amount of trust to put them in the hands of God and in the hands of your spiritual brothers and sisters."

Wow, I thought. I had learned the answer to two pressing questions in my life. First, do I have to take my socks off for the foot-washing service? The answer is yes. And second, is it OK that I feel uncomfortable about doing so? The answer, again, is yes. As a matter of fact, if there isn't at least a small sense of anxiety, humility, or awkwardness, then the ritual itself may have lost its power. Indeed, trust is a hard thing for people to learn— especially those with ugly feet.

6

Why Is the Church's Family Game Night More Competitive Than a Yankees-Red Sox Series?

I'M A BASEBALL DIEHARD. Call me an addict, if you like. I've lived and died for my team, the Oakland Athletics, many times in my life. I've watched 50,000-plus fans squeal in ecstasy, only to be crushed beyond resurrection. And yet, even after overwhelming defeat, new hope always surfaces when spring training rolls around. (I don't understand how any true baseball fan *cannot* believe in life after death when they watch it occur every year.)

Baseball is great on TV, better on the radio, but it was meant to be viewed in person. There is nothing like the enormous swath of green grass, the boos and roars of the crowd, the intricacies of the scorecard, and the smell of high-fat-content food.

One of the great traditions of the sport is the old-fashioned bench-clearing brawl. Its rules are simple enough. Two players from opposing teams begin to fight, and then everyone leaps from their bench or position in the field and tries to pummel the other side. From the stands it looks like a mini-riot or a church board meeting. The baseball profession itself often refers to the phenomenon as "good sportsmanship." (Would it reflect badly on me if I admitted to enjoying an occasional brawl? They're mostly harmless—big on bravado and weak on brutality.)

The only thing I dislike about baseball—aside from the exorbitant salaries and the New York Yankees—is brawling that works its way into the stands. We call them "fan fights," and they're an altogether different monster than those bench-clearing skirmishes. Unlike the professional scraps, fan fights provide a heavy dose of bravado *and* brutality (not a healthy mix!). I can barely stand to watch. Perhaps that's because I'm a wimp when it comes to blood. The sound of fists hitting faces literally makes me dizzy, which may explain why I make a dash for the men's restroom when a fight breaks out. I can't even guess how many fan fights I've witnessed—more than I can count on one hand. But even one's too many.

Fan fights usually occur toward the end of the game. They have little to do with the events on the field and everything to do with how many beers the combatants have consumed. I've seen grown men push each other like little boys on a sandlot and large men tossed across three rows of seats. And I've even watched an unfortunate fighter dragged down a flight of stairs by his long hair. (That fight was particularly ugly, and the stadium police handcuffed both individuals and led them away, while we, the wide-eyed spectators, gave the cops a standing ovation. If I remember right, it was the only opportunity for cheering we'd had all night.)

It's easy to find a culprit to blame for such confrontations, and it's not the artery-clogging nachos. No, it's the free-flowing booze that fans guzzle down in order to wash down the artery-clogging nachos. (Why can't they simply eat apples and sip ice water? Would it destroy the integrity of the game?)

But here's an even greater mystery: Why do fan fights pop up at the church's family game night? The clashes are often just as ugly, the sense of competition often just as thick—and yet there's no beer.

I grew up in a congregation with an active social life. Church was not only the center for spiritual growth—it was also a place to have fun with other believers and their families. And for most of my formative years up to college, a highlight at our church was the monthly "Family Fun Night."

I'd like to say I went for the Christian fellowship, but that would be a partial fib. I attended for a more practical reason—two practical reasons, to be specific. First of all, I wanted to meet girls. While that may have been not too spiritual, my second reason was: I came to bond with brothers and sisters in Christ who, like me, came to love one another and play Rook. When it came to Rook, meeting girls seemed superfluous (unless, that is, the girls also played the game).

Having grown up in a denomination uneasy about card playing (more its association with gambling than the innocuous paper with cute little kings and queens and jokers), I and many like me are greatly relieved that many authority figures have deemed Rook OK. I don't really know why, because it is a card game based on suits, trumps, tricks, hands, and numbers—just like a normal deck of cards. Truth be told, only subtle differences exist between Rook and a real card deck, but good believers have learned to walk the proper tightropes. Even our pastor—as serious a Rook player as one will ever find—half-jokingly called the game "veggie poker." Like a veggie burger or a veggie hot dog, Rook offers the feel, smell, and look of the original, minus the guilt.

While I'm not great at the game itself, I'm good at holding the cards in my hand and appearing to know exactly what I'm doing. I'm also skilled at losing in the end, but that is a talent that I achieved only through ample practice. Maybe it's because of morons like me that many conscientious citizens oppose the legalization of gambling. Or perhaps it's because of imbeciles like me that Las Vegas rivals Walt Disney World for entertainment dollars.

Fortunately, I don't mind losing. Like scrubbing the scum off the sides of the bathtub, losing is a necessary part of a greater pleasure. (Given a choice, however, I'd rather lose at Rook than scrub soap scum, but that could just be me.) Don't get me wrong; I like to win, especially when I sense I'm up against Rook aficionados who think no one aside from themselves has mastered the nuances of the game. Such card-wielding savants deserve to lose, and I happily accept my Christian calling to trump their tricks and trounce them badly. I don't rub it in their faces or anything, though I've been known to slam my cards onto the table and shout, "I'm the man!" And just as I'm beginning to stomp on my opponent's precious Rook card—which I always prefer to play low—I then demonstrate genuine Christian love by leaping onto the table and demonstrating my victory dance.

OK, so maybe it's a good thing that I don't win very often!

Unfortunately, not everyone at our church shared my—uh—detached view of defeat. For some, losing a hand was like losing a limb (no pun intended). Losing a game was even worse, like being trounced in the Super Bowl or giving away a lottery ticket that turned out to be the $100 million winner.

Part of the reason I lost so frequently was the skill and proficiency of Mr. Conrad and Mr. Small, two well-liked, well-mannered members of our church. Indeed, they knew the game like a little boy knows dirt (or maybe that's just my boy).

One could not imagine a more unflappable pair than Mr. Conrad and Mr. Small. They were generous, always giving of their invaluable time at work bees and school bake sales. Each had kids who attended the church's grade school, and one would be hard-pressed to find two more devoted dads. Their houses were frequent hangouts for the local neighborhood kids, and one felt truly fortunate to be invited into their homes for an after-church lunch. In short, they were good guys. As far as I could tell, they had only one weakness, which is a lot fewer than I have. Their weakness, however—or should I say "fatal flaw"—was Rook. But not just Rook—they were competitive in all games and sports. (Playing flag football with them was nothing short of terrifying.) But each claimed Rook as his claim to fame, which meant that every Family Fun Night was a challenge to their self-image.

One Saturday night—Family Fun Night was always on a Saturday night—everything seemed to be living up to the name of the event. There were plenty of families and, more important, one big family of God. Best of all, everyone was having fun—which was, after all, the event's middle name.

The evening's ritual was always the same. (Alas, our congregation, like most others, found something that worked, then did it that way ever after.) First, the women laid out enormous quantities of lentil loaf, Special K loaf, potato chip loaf, and other varieties that one could not possibly fathom, all on a long buffet table. The casserole dishes remained on the table throughout the evening, so participants could come and go as their stomachs demanded. In the gymnasium some played volleyball or badminton, and a few—me included—would lean against the wall and try to impress the girls. (As an overachieving young teen, I never could understand why none ever seemed dazzled by my presence. In retrospect, I should have played volleyball. Back then, however, I reasoned that volleyball might mess up my hair—carefully feathered back in a classic early-1980s manner.)

After food and volleyball (and the boys' miserable attempts at attracting the attention of the girls), most people filed into the multipurpose room—we never shied from that description—for table games. I, of course, made my way to the round table where the Rook players gathered.

We called ourselves the "Rooksters," or as one player with a thick Romanian accent said, the "rock stars."

I think the other Rooksters liked having me along, because even if they were having a bad night, at least they could have me to trounce. Not yet able to grasp their intentions, I just figured they enjoyed my corny sense of humor. I persuaded myself that it wasn't just my pitiful Rook skills that made them laugh.

One particular night Mr. Conrad and Mr. Small seemed revved up more than usual—I'm not sure why, even to this day. Maybe one had thrown down the gauntlet and made bold claims about his skill, but that wouldn't have been atypical. Everyone at the table could feel the added tension. Miss Jan, the church's Bible instructor and the most unflappable person on the planet, let alone our congregation, said, "Let's not forget that this is just a game. It doesn't matter who wins or loses." Everyone stared at her, and the silence felt dreadful. Then she looked up with a smile and said, "Of course, that shouldn't prevent me from stomping on you all tonight, but I promise not to gloat or anything."

Everyone laughed, and the tension lifted. Except for Mr. Conrad and Mr. Small, who were quieter than usual. They eyed each other nervously.

The first few rounds went to Miss Jan. I thought to myself, *Boy, she wasn't kidding. She's walking all over us.* My current theory is that she was always the best player, but she liked to let others win. That day, however, she felt it wise to win so that neither Mr. Conrad nor Mr. Small could.

Believe it or not, even I won a round, which I took to be a sign that perhaps God was looking out for our Family Fun Night, working very hard (to the point of creating a few miracles) to keep Mr. Conrad and Mr. Small from triumphing.

Toward the end Mr. Small had won the bid and was rapidly scoring hand after hand. I felt torn, because I was his called partner for the round. It was my "duty" to help him win, but I didn't have to do much, because Mr. Small had been dealt the sweetest hand I've ever seen. Mr. Conrad was visibly annoyed. At one point he pounded his fist on the table and muttered, "Who shuffled these stupid cards?" Apparently, he'd forgotten that *he* had been the guilty party.

I knew that something would blow if one or the other won, so I took matters into my own hand—no pun intended. I was holding a very high and a very low trump card. I knew that my one high card guaranteed Mr. Small's first and probably only victory for the night. Then he played a low trump card and glanced at me. The look was clear enough. It meant that it was now the time to play that high trump card.

Some were already out of trump, but a few still had some cards to play, and they were higher than Mr. Small's. To my right Miss Jan played a 10 and muttered, "Well, that's about the best I can do."

I looked at my hand. I had a 13 and a 5. If I played the 13, we would easily take all the remaining cards, and Mr. Small would win. I played the 5, giving the hand to Miss Jan.

Mr. Small immediately threw his cards on the table and stared at me. "What were you thinking? Have you ever played this game?"

Mr. Conrad, likely delighted at the turn in events, said, "Take it easy on the boy. He played the best he could."

Mr. Small turned to Mr. Conrad and said, "Oh, and I bet you really enjoyed that, didn't you?"

"A little bit," Mr. Conrad replied, all of us wishing that he hadn't.

Before I realized what was happening, Mr. Small leaped onto Mr. Conrad, and they were rolling on the floor in a tight embrace. Miss Jan started to cry. Some of the men ran to them and tried to separate them, but neither would relent. I thought about the brutal fights I'd seen at the ballpark and decided that this topped them all.

Soon the Conrad kids were squabbling with the Small kids over whose dad was tougher. Then the friends of the Conrad kids started to taunt the friends of the Small kids. All in all, it was Family Not-So-Fun Night.

No one got hurt, although two large egos seemed a bit battered. Plus it humiliated the wife of each rival, though not as much as their kids, who had to live with the incident at school on Monday. I wondered how the church would react to their behavior. When kids caused major fights at our school, often someone got suspended for a few days. But I couldn't imagine the pastor suspending Mr. Conrad or Mr. Small from church, at least not because of a silly brawl over Rook. (OK, there are no silly fights over Rook.) Besides, how can you suspend them from church when it seemed as if that was exactly where they needed to be?

Make no mistake, some members were ready to have both Mr. Conrad and Mr. Small—along with their feisty children—permanently booted from church. How can one allow two ticking time bombs to walk the aisles of our sacred sanctuary? What if both were taking up the offering—as they often did—and one collected more money than the other? Would there be a bench-clearing brawl—or is it a pew-clearing brawl?

Most of the women in the congregation felt that, at minimum, the church should ban both Mr. Conrad and Mr. Small from Family Fun Night. And those who opposed even such moderate measures believed they should not be allowed to play Rook anymore.

The pastor, however, remained strangely silent on the issue, which most chalked up as evidence that he was devoid of a spine.

The next weekend, with the matter yet to be resolved, the pastor's sermon took us to the upper room less than 24 hours before Christ's gruesome crucifixion. The disciples, he reminded us, were bickering, or at least we can easily imagine they were. It's never a stretch to conceive of the disciples fighting, because it seems as if that's all they did throughout the Gospels. They squabbled over who would be the greatest and over who would ultimately sit by Jesus when He became king. Probably they argued over what to eat for dinner, over who cast out the most demons, and over who would win the chariot-racing Super Bowl. All of them were about as competitive as a bunch of drunken Yankees fans in Fenway Park (or is it drunk Red Sox fans in Yankee Stadium?). Or even worse, they were about as competitive as Mr. Conrad and Mr. Small.

So what did Jesus do?

He could have booted them out of the disciple club or made them sit in the corner for a time-out. Perhaps He could have heaped a nasty hellfire-and-brimstone sermon on them. But instead, He did something radical.

First, Jesus took off His robe. Then He picked up a basin of water and a towel. Of course, the disciples were astonished and a bit embarrassed. After all, Jesus was doing slave work. The man they hoped would soon be king bent down and washed their dirty, stinky feet. (The streets were full of raw sewage in those days, remember.)

The rest, as they say, is history—or is it eucharistic theology? Jesus managed to turn the most important Jewish holiday into the quintessential Christian ritual by applying new meaning to the bread and wine of Passover. But most people today end the story there and forget the crucial words that followed.

Knowing that He had only a few moments left with His disciples, Jesus said, "A new command I give you: Love one another. As I have loved you, so you must love one another. By this all men will know that you are my disciples, if you love one another" (John 13:34).

Our pastor, after his brief homily about loving one another as Jesus loves us, encouraged us to move to special rooms for a foot-washing service. "Don't take this lightly, and don't simply wash the foot of a good friend," he urged us. "Find someone you may have been at odds with."

Instantly every head jerked in the direction of Mr. Conrad and Mr. Small, both of whom sat staring at their feet.

In the room set aside for men I washed the feet of an older man I barely knew. (As I've made abundantly clear, the foot-washing experience is often a harrowing one for me, but my partner made me feel at ease. What's more, his feet were nearly as hideous as mine, which allowed me to relax further.)

But as we resolutely relived the upper room encounter, I looked in the corner and—no surprise—there were Mr. Conrad and Mr. Small. What was startling, however, was that they were smiling, even laughing together. They prayed for each other and hugged each other. That was shocking enough, but what flabbergasted us most was that they and their families sat together in church following the foot-washing service.

Simply shrugging it off, I muttered, "We'll see how long this lasts. Just wait until the next Rook tourney."

A few weeks lumbered past, and Family Fun Night arrived again. The Conrads and the Smalls were still friends, and rumor had it that they'd spent a Saturday evening together playing Rook and watching *The Love Boat*. (Many will recall—shamefully, perhaps—that it was once fashionable to eat popcorn and watch *The Love Boat* on Saturday nights.)

At that very next Family Fun Night the same routines played themselves out—first the variety of strange casseroles, next the volleyball, then the games. I found my seat at the Rooksters' table, but Mr. Conrad and Mr. Small never joined us. After a few dismal rounds (it wasn't the same without them), I searched the multipurpose room for our wayward card players. They were at a corner table playing Mouse Trap with the kids.

Miss Jan worked up the courage to invite both men to join us, but they turned us down. "We decided that it would be best to love one another," Mr. Small explained, "and if we can't do it playing Rook, we'll settle for Mouse Trap."

While Mouse Trap's a great game, I thought they were misinterpreting the pastor's sermon and the point of Jesus' command. Christ never said, "Love one another by giving up Rook."

Mr. Conrad glanced at Miss Jan and said, "We'll join you Rooksters soon, but for now we have fences to mend."

For a few months they played games considerably more benign than Rook, such as Uno and Skip-Bo and Pit. Mostly they played with the kids, helping to teach them to be good sports and to participate just "for the fun of it." To be honest, it seemed as if they were having so much fun that we Rooksters felt a bit jealous.

Eventually they did play Rook again. They were still competitive and still took the game seriously. But they never fought again, either with each other or with us. Mr. Small apologized to me for his outburst, and I apologized for causing him to lose. When I did, he replied, "I knew it! I knew you did that on purpose, because not even you are that bad at Rook."

I laughed and said, "Maybe one day I'll be as good at the game as you and Mr. Conrad."

Mr. Small stared at me and declared, "I guess we're all entitled to wishful thinking." We both laughed.

And I can't think of anyone after that who embodied Jesus' new command better than Mr. Conrad and Mr. Small.

7

What's a Father to Do in the Mothers' Room?

HAVING SAID WHAT I have about kids in church, I must also acknowledge that the mothers' room is a great invention, on a par with the Popsicle and the epidural. It's ideal for mothers who would like to listen to the service but don't feel comfortable breast feeding in public. I'm sure I wouldn't, but then again, I'm a man, and that would certainly cause heads to turn. Plus, the room is often filled with toys, games, and puzzles, and sometimes it's just better to let the kids play rather than to inflict a long lecture on them.

Most churches pipe the audio from the main sanctuary into the mothers' room so they can listen to the service while taking care of their children. A well-equipped church—usually newer than 1965—will offer glass windows that allow the mothers to see the service. The truly forward-thinking, high-tech churches will have one-way glass on the windows so the mothers can see out, but no one else can peer in.

But today we live in a "liberated" society that mixes and matches gender roles. For example, my mom gripes that she can count on one hand how many diapers my dad changed. I've had days in which I changed more diapers than a single hand can count, which either demonstrates that I'm a helpful father or that my son is prolific—or maybe even both.

Not too long after Ramsey's birth, Michelle and I would attend church with him neatly wrapped in a blanket like a small burrito. We garnered the expected oohs and aahs, and it was amazing to watch full-grown, otherwise articulate people speak in high-pitched goo-goo talk. I wondered how these silly grown-ups must have looked from Ramsey's perspective. Most likely by this point he was convinced that all grown-ups talked that way.

Ramsey was still breast-feeding, which was a slight problem. In general, Michelle rarely minded serving up lunch in public, unless we were in a quiet place. One of Ramsey's more annoying quirks was the overpowering sucking noise he could generate while eating. I always thought each gulp sounded like a sliding glass door in desperate need of oil, but Michelle compared it to wet rubber boots sliding across linoleum. Either way, whether it was a sliding glass door or a boot squeak, Ramsey's deafening eating habits made it nearly impossible for Michelle to remain in church for the entire service, and she often wound up in the mothers' room.

To me the mothers' room was a place of mystery. I wondered what happened behind those closed doors. Was it an excuse to gather and share the latest gossip? Was it a secret feminist meeting place? Did they discuss how they could subvert the centuries of male-dominated discourse in the church?

The sermon had barely started when Ramsey suddenly woke from a deep sleep and was hungry. We could tell when he was famished, because he would pucker up like a goldfish, and if he didn't receive almost instantaneous satisfaction, he would scream as if the world would end at that moment. No doubt he believed it would.

I gave Michelle a glance that attempted to convey my sympathies. Obviously, I reasoned, it was time for a feeding, which meant it was time for her to enter the mysterious mothers' room. I patted her hand gently and said, "I'm sorry. Is there anything I can do?"

When I asked, "Is there anything I can do?" I didn't mean "Is there anything I can do?" That's simply what all men—especially fathers—say when they hope there is nothing they can do. Michelle, however, never got that memo. She smiled and reached into our stylish diaper bag. Then, as she looked up at me, she pulled out a bottle with mother's milk in it. (I tried to remember what diabolical person had given us a breast pump for a gift.)

"I just want to enjoy church for once," she announced. "Would you mind feeding him this time?"

Suddenly I started to panic. Looking around the sanctuary, then at her, I asked, "Where should I take him?"

"To the mothers' room, of course."

The mothers' room? This was obviously a cruel joke, perhaps an early April Fools' Day surprise, which is what made it such a good surprise, since it wasn't April Fools' Day. "They call it the *'mothers'* room' for a reason, Michelle," I protested. "I can't go in there."

She looked genuinely surprised at my reaction—I'm sure I resembled a horse that had just glimpsed a rattlesnake. "Go on," she insisted. "There's probably no one in there anyway. I bet you'll be all by yourself."

Not having considered that possibility, I felt better about it. I picked up the little burrito and headed for the mothers' room.

The door was closed, but I couldn't miss the fact that it did not say "fathers' room." Of course, neither did it say "no fathers allowed," but that might simply be assumed. With the diaper bag slung over my shoulder and Ramsey cradled in one arm (ah, the days when I could hold him with one arm and not get tired), I turned the knob to enter the enigmatic region.

Inside I could hear children laughing, which made me hesitate. Where there were children laughing, I reasoned, there were probably mothers chatting—mothers who would stare at me as if to say, "What's *he* doing here?" Maybe there would be screams, as if I'd mistakenly walked into the women's restroom.

When I peeked into the room, it for the most part looked just as I had imagined. Toys were scattered across the floor like a posthurricane news photo. Five kids clustered around a puzzle, tinkering with the pieces and becoming frustrated. Right by the door two little girls in frilly dresses were playing with Barbie dolls, so I said, "Are you playing with Barbies?" (Why is it that adults feel obligated to ask children the most obvious questions?) One of the girls, somewhat horrified at my question, glanced up at me and said, "This isn't Barbie! It's Mary Magdalene!"

I tried to keep a straight face, but failed. "She's wearing pretty modern clothes for Mary Magdalene, but then again, she always was hip on fashion," I commented.

"That's right," the rather precocious girl said. "She was a hooker. Do you know what a hooker is?"

"Susan!" A voice from the corner of the room ended our charming conversation before it could hardly begin. Relieved, I looked up and saw four mothers talking in the far corner. One was breast-feeding a baby, but she fortunately had a blanket over her. The other three were simply talking, so I assumed the other children who were playing with puzzles belonged to them. "Susan has quite an imagination," said the one woman who seemed to be the ringleader of the four.

I laughed and waved my hands as if to say, "No need to worry about offending me, of all people."

Just then I noticed a man sitting in the corner opposite the four women. He was gently rocking a small baby who was deeply sleeping. Though I'd never seen him before, I felt as if I'd run into a hometown friend in a foreign land. Immediately I sat by the man.

When he looked up at me, his face said it all. He felt just as I did. "So you've been exiled to the mothers' room as well?" he said with a smile.

"Yep," I replied as I slipped the bottle's nipple into Ramsey's puckered-up mouth. He started sucking the milk out, and the sliding glass door began to grind. (Truth is, the more I listened to him, the more I agreed that he mimicked the squeak of a wet rubber boot.) I thought to myself, *I sure hope he loses that earsplitting squeak before he starts dating.* Out loud I said, "Don't ask me why, but my wife actually wanted to get something out of the church service. Have you ever heard such nonsense?"

I was kidding, of course, but I'm not sure he caught the humor. "Well, don't you think she's entitled to that once in a while?"

"Yes, of course, I mean, well, I was only—never mind!" There's nothing more futile than trying to explain a bad joke.

Just then the ringleader woman in the corner tried to get our attention, which startled both of us. "You know, you fellas are welcome to join us over here. This isn't an exclusive club."

"Well, that's not what the door says," I wanted to say. "It declares 'mothers' room,' which can be interpreted as 'This is an exclusive gathering of mothers, and fathers need not apply.'" Fortunately, I thought better of it.

We grabbed our kids and our chairs and moved over to their side of the room. They all looked at Ramsey and said, "He looks just like you."

"Yes, the poor kid," I answered. "Maybe after a little therapy or plastic surgery he'll recover."

They laughed, and one said, "Or maybe he'll just get his mother's brains." Then they all really laughed—a deep-gut laugh that must have been audible outside the room.

Ouch, I thought at first. Then I had to agree. If the poor boy was to be saddled with my looks, he had better have his mother's brains or he'd never survive.

Ramsey was chugging steadily along on his bottle when he started to cough. I immediately put him over my shoulder and gently patted his back. Ramsey then burped—a deep-bass burp that would have made any college dormitory male proud. But the burp was merely a warning of bad things to come. In a swift jerk Ramsey spit up his entire lunch. It wasn't the kind of gentle drool that hardly counts for much, but a full-on vomit that ran down my back and drenched me in a foul smell.

One of the onlooking mothers said, "You know, you ought to put a towel or blanket over your shoulder before you do that. You'll save a lot on your dry-cleaning bill."

Everyone laughed as I tried to reach unreachable parts of my back with a dry towel. One of the mothers finally felt sorry enough for me to help wipe off the bodily fluids I couldn't reach.

I tried to defend myself, stammering, "Yes, I usually do, but I just wasn't thinking." Then I added, looking at my shoulder and down my back, "I'm sure Michelle's going to love this."

Without warning I heard a gurgling sound like a geyser about to spray. Then erupted a noise like a hissing cat. I looked at Ramsey, whose face had turned dark red like a pomegranate, and I knew that he had just made my job a lot tougher. Groaning, I reached into the diaper bag for a diaper and muttered, "We're coming apart at both ends now, aren't we?"

The others in the room chuckled, and one said, "Must not be feeling well, I bet."

"Oh, he'll be all right," I said.

"I don't mean the baby—I was referring to his dad." They all laughed especially hard, and even the other man was so treasonous as to join the mirth.

I lifted Ramsey over to the changing table, but he seemed wigglier than usual—and messier. But the real problem was stage fright: I simply was having a difficult time performing the art of diaper changing in front of such obvious experts. I tried to think of comforting passages from the Bible, such as 1 Peter 4:12: "Beloved, do not think it strange concerning the fiery trial which is to try you, as though some strange thing happened to you" (NKJV). No doubt, this counted as a "fiery trial." Perhaps, I reasoned, this was what that passage in Daniel really meant by the "time of trouble." Then Psalm 55:22 went through my mind: "Cast your burden on the Lord, and He shall sustain you; He shall never permit the righteous to be moved" (NKJV). Well, he certainly had allowed Ramsey to be moved, but I'm sure that wasn't what the text meant.

At last I wrapped the diaper around Ramsey's waist, fastened the sticky tabs, and put on a one-piece jumper. I considered raising my hands in victory like a rodeo cowboy after roping a calf and tying its legs, but instead I reached for the heavy diaper and started carrying it to the diaper pail. Don't ask me why—call it nerves on my part—but the diaper slipped from my hand and landed on the carpet, and let's just say that "splattered" is a good word for what transpired a split second afterward.

As I stared in horror at the mess, one of the women said, "You know, you ought to make sure the diaper is tightly wrapped up before you carry it. It'll save you a lot of grief."

"And a lot of smell," another added as they all laughed.

One of the women was kind enough to hold Ramsey while I grabbed a wad of paper towels. It took me about 10 minutes to clean the mess, but the smell never left the room. However, no one seemed to mind the unsightly stain or the stench, and I assumed they were all too accustomed to both.

Almost as if on cue, as soon as I had cleaned the mess Ramsey began to cry. It wasn't a hold-your-head-back-and-howl cry, but it was enough to make the woman who was holding him eager to hand him off to me. Unfortunately, I was out of milk and had no desire to get Michelle and ruin her rare church experience. Besides, I didn't want her to think I was a wimp and couldn't handle a mere half hour in the mothers' room.

First I tried rocking him back and forth, but he continued to cry. I would stick my pinky in his mouth, and he'd suck on it for a few moments. But as soon as he realized that he couldn't squeeze anything tasty out of the finger, he would cry again. I tried singing to him, but that elicited a more urgent cry—and probably drove the four mothers and one father crazy.

At last Ramsey closed his eyes and fell asleep almost as quickly as he had begun to cry. I sat in one of the rocking chairs and exhaled. For the first time I realized that the pastor's voice was booming from a round speaker on the ceiling. The sound was thin, like an old AM radio, but I could understand him well enough. He was offering his closing prayer, which meant that I had heard nothing of his sermon. If asked, I couldn't even have identified his topic, let alone cite any of his points.

"At least Michelle got to enjoy the service," I said loud enough for everyone to hear, "because I can say without lying that I did not."

Then the ringleader mother proclaimed, "Welcome to the club. You are now officially dubbed a mothers' room mother."

I tried to decide if that was a compliment. When I realized it was, I said, "Great! Do I get a medal or at least a golden diaper?"

"No, you simply get the satisfaction of being a good mommy."

"Well," I responded, "I'm having a tough enough time just being a father. I don't think I'm cut out to be a mother."

After the service Michelle met me in the mothers' room. I must have looked terrible, like a soldier returning from an all-night raid, because she asked, "Are you all right?"

"Couldn't be better," I said a little sarcastically. "I bet you didn't know that I'm now an official mothers' room mother."

"Was it all that bad?" Michelle asked.

"No," I sighed. "Actually, it was informative."

"How so?"

"First of all, I at last know what goes on behind closed doors in the mysterious mothers' room. That discovery alone may have been worth the trouble. And second, I fully grasp that the most underappreciated member of the church is the mothers' room mother."

And the ringleader mother said, "Yes, but now he's one of us."

Why Was Sabbath School More Fun When I Was a Kid?

I LOVED SABBATH SCHOOL as a little boy. The kids in my neighborhood thought my family was weird for attending church on a Saturday (many assumed we were Jewish), and they were equally horrified that I was missing Saturday morning cartoons. How could I go through life without a weekly quota of Bugs Bunny? But as far as I was concerned, Sabbath school topped Bugs Bunny, Tom and Jerry, and Woody Woodpecker combined. It was, quite honestly, the highlight of my week.

For those not familiar with "Sabbath school," think of it as Sunday school on Saturday. I grew up attending (and still attend) a Seventh-day Adventist church. (Actually, we started going when I was about 7, so my memories of those years are vivid.) In the Adventist tradition, we worship on Saturdays. We call it "Sabbath," because we strongly believe that we are following in a tradition of Sabbath observance that began when God rested on the seventh day of Creation. (Oh, and then there's the whole fourth commandment thing—"Remember the Sabbath day by keeping it holy" [Exodus 20:8]—that we've never taken to be a trifling point.)

I couldn't wait for Sabbath school to come. My two sisters and I loved it so much that we would play it on Friday nights in anticipation. (So-called normal children watched TV, rode bikes, or played Monopoly on Friday nights, but we were—and still are—happily abnormal.) Then on Sabbath afternoons we'd reenact the morning's Sabbath school—with our own added twists, of course. I would always sprinkle in a few commercials, imagining that our Sabbath school was a kind of radio or TV variety show. (Somehow, as a young child, I felt that the only thing Sabbath school lacked was the occasional pitch for toilet paper or carpet cleaner.)

As an 8- or 9-year-old boy I never felt so welcomed as when I'd step into our Sabbath school room, gaudily decorated with butterflies, clouds, flowers, and birds. Mr. Cendejas would stand among the clouds—cotton balls glued to cloud-shaped construction paper—and greet us as if we were long lost relatives: "Mike, you came! So glad to have you!" To me it was a thrill to be thought of so highly by a grown-up.

My mom, the leader of our Sabbath school, played the piano and led the singing. Because she comes from the old-time gospel tradition, she performed loudly and flamboyantly—the kind of piano playing that says if you aren't hitting all the keys, you aren't really trying. Best of all, we sang such favorites as "Joshua Fought the Battle of Jericho," "Only a Boy Named David," and "He's Got the Whole World in His Hands."

And we didn't just sing—oh, no! That would have been too easy. My mom insisted that we add choreography to the words. She believed that we weren't really singing if we sat on our tiny plastic chairs and shouted, "If you're happy and you know it, clap your hands." No, we had to be on our feet clapping, crouching, bending, kicking, or waving. Singing was a whole-body, whole-mind, nothing-saved-for-tomorrow event. Granted, she did not allow hip-swinging or joggling, because that might be construed as dancing, but we were allowed to wave our arms, clap our hands, and march in place. (The marching came perilously close to dancing, but my mom hoped no one would notice.)

After the singing we would pray. Miss Vesta often did the praying, and somehow we believed that because she was old and because her voice had a slight quiver, her prayers were more potent. She had been praying for a long time, we reasoned, so she must have been well rehearsed. When we told her our prayer requests—the usual appeals for new puppies, new babies, parents to get along, and grandmas to survive illnesses—we really, *really* believed that God was listening. Most important, we somehow knew that if God forgot to hear or if He was too busy to listen, He'd get an earful from Miss Vesta, and not even God could want that!

After prayer we always played a game. My favorite was Bible baseball, but that was because I loved anything that involved baseball—except for the New York Yankees. (My almost obsessive dislike of the Yankees began early in life and has yet to wane!) We'd play in teams, boys against the girls.

67

It was a kind of trivia game, and we could choose what type of question we wanted—a single, double, triple, or home run. The girls were wimps, and they always opted for singles. Of course, those questions were easier than triples, so they got most of them right and scored lots of runs. The boys, on the other hand, would aim for a home run every time. After we boys made three quick misses, the girls would be up again.

On special occasions our Sabbath school would make a craft. It's amazing how spiritual a few Popsicle sticks can be, especially when there's Elmer's glue and glitter on the table. And whoever invented construction paper and Crayola crayons deserves bonus stars on his or her crown. Miss Vesta always tried to find a correlation between the craft and the day's lesson, but sometimes it was a stretch. Once, when we learned about how Moses crossed the Red Sea, we made rafts out of Popsicle sticks. She reasoned that if God hadn't worked a miracle, they would have been forced to construct rafts. (Well, it wasn't very biblical, but we still had fun making the rafts.)

Once in a while our Sabbath school would take a brief excursion into the grown-ups' Sabbath school to watch a multimedia program called *Mission Spotlight*. It was better than the Learning Channel because, well, there was no such thing as the Learning Channel back then. Each slide program focused on the specific region of the world that would benefit from our Sabbath school offering. The logic was (and still is) that if we could only see the hardships and the triumphs in the area, it would motivate us to give more. It worked for me. I pulled up every couch cushion in our house in search of loose change so I could help build another bamboo schoolhouse. (At times I felt like an archaeologist digging through ancient ruins, though the artifacts I found included half-eaten peanut butter sandwiches, pens, and keys, as well as pennies.)

As I watched *Mission Spotlight* it always amazed me how popular "Jesus Loves Me" was. No matter where the *Mission Spotlight* cameras ventured, they managed to find children who would sing the song loudly and in a funny language. Then it dawned on me that maybe *my* language is the funny one. (Today I realize how true that is!) I even wondered if children from other nations actually knew any other songs, because that seemed to be the extent of their repertoire. I determined to sing as loud as they did. If they could live in grass huts, go to church in cement-block boxes, and sing the same song again and again, then I had no excuse but to be a little happier. After all, I lived in a normal house, went to church in a fancier box, and could sing more than one song. I was blessed.

The highlight of Sabbath school was "lesson study." The name of it— "lesson study"—sounds dull and academic, but it was absolutely engaging. Presenting it was Mr. Cendejas's special talent. Each week he would take a story from the Bible and recount it in the most imaginative way. He was a brilliant storyteller. For four years I heard Mr. Cendejas present nearly every major Bible story. With stories from Creation to the book of Revelation, he made the characters truly real, as if they were friends—or wicked enemies.

To this day the pictures he created in my mind during Sabbath school are the mental images that flash through my mind when I read my Bible. Although I come from a Ukrainian-Russian-German-French-etc. background, I may as well have been Jewish, since the Bible's stories were now my family's stories. (Maybe, in a spiritual sense, I was and am Jewish.)

At the close of Sabbath school we'd clasp hands, form a circle around the room, and sing one last song. Holding hands still, we'd close our eyes and pray for each other. Then we'd groan, knowing we had to go to church. Not that church was horrible (and not that it was great, either); it just could never live up to Sabbath school.

Unfortunately, something appallingly tragic happened. I walked out of Sabbath school one day only to discover that I was no longer a kid. It was a terrible realization, and I don't wish it on anyone. I had worked my way up the so-called ranks, up through Sabbath schools geared for older and older kids. What I didn't realize—but do now—is that the entire process was simply laying the groundwork for something I never believed could happen to me: I'd have to attend adult Sabbath school.

In many ways it was not fair. Someone should have been telling us from the get-go that this meaningful, exciting, and rousing thing called "Sabbath school" has a way of evolving into a more sedate service that some have sarcastically called "prechurch" or "church number 2" or "Oh no, not (groan) another church service."

No doubt someone reading this is muttering, "He can't say that about Sabbath school." My response may sound flippant, but it's true nonetheless: "Why not, when nearly everyone else is at least *thinking* it."

I've had the privilege of traveling around North America, and I've seen hundreds of Sabbath schools. Most adult Sabbath schools follow essentially the same formula.

First a chorister stands at the podium and welcomes the scattered few spread haphazardly throughout the main sanctuary. Next he or she invites the faithful few to "open your hymnals to hymn number 274." Well, it might be hymn number 543 or 123, but the point is the same. Then for the opening song, he or she asks the slightly larger gathering to stand and sing hymn number 431.

After the opening hymn—first and last verse only, of course—the Sabbath school superintendent (sounds very CEO-like, doesn't it?) steps up to the podium to welcome the now marginally bigger group. He or she offers a few announcements, gives a *Cliff Notes* version of what to expect from the morning's service, and sits down.

Occasionally a third person will step up to the podium in order to read a mission story. First, however, he or she must offer a third welcome before beginning to read. If the reader's a skilled one, the experience is tolerable, even gratifying. But if the person lacks inflection or articulation, the experience can be as maddening as Chinese water torture. While reading the mission story is rarely as exciting as a firsthand account or *Mission Spotlight,* it is infinitely better than another report from the Sabbath school treasurer about the Sabbath school offering totals. (But then again, that may just be me.)

While the story is still fresh in the minds of the listeners, the Sabbath school collects an offering. (The meeting could not have "officially" taken place without some kind of offering, so it's crucial that the superintendent not forget it.) Inevitably in our church, however, the offering plates wind up missing. Once someone has located them, the superintendent asks, "Will the ushers please rise?" As if they'd been asked to mow the lawn during the fourth quarter of the Rose Bowl, the ushers reluctantly stand and glance around the room to make sure they're not the only ones on their feet. Then the superintendent prays.

If a church is especially fortunate, there will be a special musical selection. Our church seems to reserve this time for the more unusual musicians—the musical saw player, the accordionist, and the whistler—the ones who might seem out of place during the worship service. I always figured that every church had a musical saw player, an accordionist, and a whistler, but it was only when I began to travel the country that I realized how truly blessed we were.

The adult Sabbath school ends by dividing into groups for "lesson study," often a hit-or-miss proposition. The right teacher can create a dynamic study group, but a dull one can turn a potentially stimulating session into a half hour of tortuous tedium, like meeting with the IRS about how to avoid an audit. If the church is small enough, there may be no options for lesson study groups, in which case a single individual takes on the role of a faux pastor preaching a simulated sermon.

I'm a dad now, and lately I've spent more Sabbath school time with 3- and 4-year-olds than with the grown-ups, but I don't mind. The formula for my little boy's Sabbath school is not that different from when I was a boy, and he squeals with ecstasy when we announce that we are going to Sabbath school. Sometimes he wakes up on a Tuesday or Wednesday morning and the first thing out of his mouth is, "Are we going to Sabbath school?" When we tell him no, he looks about as crushed as a wine grape. I'll admit, it's not as intellectually satisfying for me as it was when I was a boy, but Ramsey likes it better than *VeggieTales,* and that's really saying something!

Fortunately, my denomination puts out some stupendous materials to help people put together interesting Sabbath schools. And while I have no interest in telling people how they must conduct them (remember the adage about "different strokes"), my return into the rites of Sabbath school for kids leads me to ask a slew of questions about how we do it for grown-ups.

Recalling how good it felt to be greeted as a boy by Mr. Cendejas, I wonder, How would people respond if everyone were greeted by name? Yes, four or five routine welcomes from the up-front podium is nice, but nothing beats a personal handshake. I've often believed that part of the reason bars and pubs are so popular is that the customers and staff know each other by name—think of the theme song from the old television program *Cheers.* Why can't the same be true of Sabbath school? If someone went out of her way to come to Sabbath School, why not greet her by name? What if Sabbath school greeted people with the kind of infectious enthusiasm that inspired them to want to arrive on time?

And what about the singing? Singing is largely what made Sabbath school exciting for us kids. It was loud and active and lively. Interestingly, I've searched Psalms—the Bible's hymnbook—and have yet to find a single example of quiet worship in a corporate setting. If the people came together as a body in the Bible, the worship was alive, loud, and lively—kind of like Sabbath school for kids.

And what about prayer? Prayer was more than a ritual when I was a kid. It was a direct connection to God, and we believed without a trace of doubt that He would answer. Whatever happened to that faith? What if it found its way into grown-ups' Sabbath schools?

Speaking of Bible games, why can't we still play a friendly bout of Bible Baseball among adults? (OK, I may be the only one who's in favor of this one!)

And last, what about the lesson study? The stories of our childhood still stick with us, while we're hard-pressed to recall in the afternoon what we discussed just that morning. Why not return to the stories? If I remember right, Jesus' primary method of teaching was narrative. Maybe He knew something about how to make wisdom and insight stick? Maybe He understood something that our children—and their Sabbath school leaders—also know: stories never leave us.

I have no desire to go back to children's Sabbath school. I don't want to be talked to as a child, treated as a child, or entertained like a child. As Paul wrote: "When I was child, I talked like a child, I thought like a child, I reasoned like a child." But just as with Paul, I grew up and "put childish ways behind me" (1 Corinthians 13:11). Yet, despite this maturity, I'm very aware of Jesus' almost intimidating words: "Unless you change and become like little children, you will never enter the kingdom of heaven" (Matthew 18:3).

OK, so Jesus wasn't talking about Sabbath school—an idea that wouldn't be invented until nearly two millennia later—but He was speaking about humbling ourselves, about approaching God as a child does, with wide eyes and absolute trust. I just hope we grown-ups don't lose that sense of wonder that I see every time I take my little boy to Sabbath school. And if we have lost that wonder, I hope we'll do whatever it takes—even changing our Sabbath school formats—to get it back.

9

Why Must the Church's Work Bee Always Happen When I Have Tickets on the 50-Yard Line?

OUR CHURCH DESPERATELY NEEDED a gymnasium. Instead, we had a bread box for a building that had originally housed the Pathfinder Club, and even *it* felt claustrophobic when reciting the JMV—does anyone remember the Junior Missionary Volunteers?—Pledge within its walls. The building was tiny and plain like a very large shed or an enormous brick. And yet it was practically a historical landmark as far as we were concerned, because Mrs. Kindopp, one of our church's matriarchs, had donated it to the church shortly after Noah set his animals free.

Officially the building went by the title "Kindopp Hall." Unofficially we called it "The Firetrap," "The Mold-Maker," or "The Make-out Hideout." It gained the latter name for its notoriety as a great place for a starry-eyed couple to hide behind and to kiss. To be honest, I'm not sure anyone actually did, because at our school the penalties were stiff for couples caught in the act of PDA—public displays of affection. When rumors circulated that some couple had been kissing behind the building, the truth would eventually win out and we'd be disappointed.

Despite the jokes, the old building was solid as a rock (like a boxy loaf of stale bread). It just needed a face-lift and a good scrubbing (and a camera placed behind it to catch smooching couples, if there were any). Even more, it needed to be about five times bigger to fulfill its necessary duties.

For as long as I could remember, members at our church talked about constructing a new gymnasium, but they did so in hushed tones, as if Kindopp Hall might hear them and be offended. Some worried that if they erected a larger, more useful structure to replace Kindopp Hall, the old building might not receive the repair it needed and would—horrors!—be razed. Even advocates for a new building prefaced their call to action with a concern for the life of the old one.

Then one day talk turned to deeds. The school board and the church board—two separate boards consisting of the exact same people—voted a new gymnasium. It would be a grand structure made of pink cement block—the official building material of church-affiliated buildings during the early 1980s. More than just a gymnasium, the edifice would contain a large multipurpose room, five classrooms, a faculty lounge, and an office for the school's principal. Indeed, the structure would be a monument to some of the core values of our local church—good education, strong families, and dull architecture.

There was, as with all good things, a catch. While much of the skilled labor would be done by skilled laborers—i.e., contractors and trained construction people—volunteers from our church would carry out the grunt work. My dad, a major supporter of the school, volunteered himself for all the work bees. What I didn't understand then was that by volunteering himself, he was also volunteering me. It was the result of a millennia-old hierarchy that I could not defy—although I tried!

Our work bees took place on Sundays. My dad and I woke early and drove to the monolithic monstrosity everyone called "the gym." I called it a cruel way to keep me from watching the San Francisco 49ers play. Instead of enjoying another Joe Montana pass to Dwight Clark in the end zone, I shoveled gravel into a wheelbarrow, then dumped it into a pile near the garbage dumpster. I received that assignment after it became painfully clear to Mr. Lee, the work bee's organizer, who had enormous experience in construction, that I was inept at almost all other tasks. I was incompetent at laying concrete, rolling out insulation, hammering plasterboard to studs, or tiling shower room floors. Furthermore, I stunk at painting, sanding, or bricklaying. But man, if I couldn't shovel gravel!

For a mere $4.98 at Radio Shack, I purchased an AM radio with earphones so I could listen to 49er games as I shoveled and wheelbarrowed. Yet something about the massive monolithic structure interfered with radio signals. Either that, or there was a batch of nuclear waste secretly buried beneath the building. Whatever the cause, Joe Montana never reached my ears.

Toward the end of November the weather was getting cooler, and work bees became more urgent. It was crucial that the roofing work get done before the rainy season, which was bound to hit any day. The church designated the Sunday before Thanksgiving as the last thrust of work before taking a few months off. However, it was important that as many volunteers as possible show up to complete the absolutely necessary jobs before the rainy season. Of course my dad promised we'd be there, and I begrudgingly muttered, "Wouldn't miss it."

But that evening my life became a bit complicated. My close friend Joel called me and said, "Mike, you won't believe what I've got between my sticky fingers."

Not in the mood for such games, I replied in a monotone, "Let me guess: you've been raiding the cookie jar again. You rogue, you!"

"Mike, I've got two tickets to this Sunday's Niners-Rams game. And we are on the 50-yard line."

"We?" I liked the sound of that little pronoun. "Did you say 'We'? Let me grab a Q-tip so I can clean my ears, because I'm almost sure you said 'We.' Not 'I' but 'We.'"

"Yep. Of course, I'll need some cash to help pay for your ticket. Some guy was selling them in the classifieds. All I did is call, and, well, I'll pick you up about 10:00 a.m."

I was ecstatic. It was at that moment I fully appreciated two of Joel's finest traits—his resourcefulness and his recently acquired driver's license. "I'll be ready," I exclaimed.

Joel hung up, and I buried my head in my pillow so I could scream with joy without being heard. (Juvenile, I know, but one must understand: these were 49er tickets, not some semipro team, like the Cincinnati Bengals.)

I'd never been to a pro football game in person, and what a game to see first—the Niners and the Rams. (This was back in the glory days when the Rams were from Los Angeles, and all teams from Los Angeles were hated rivals to San Francisco Bay Area teams and fans.)

Then a clang of horror hit me—*thwack!* I suddenly realized that the game would take place during the church's final work bee, the important one before the rainy season. I fell onto my bed and said—speaking to the light fixture, I guess—"Why must the church's work bee take place when I've got tickets on the 50-yard line?" Months of suppressed bitterness welled up inside me. "Come to think of it, why must the church's work bee get in the way of a lot of things I'd rather do."

As I thought about it more I became increasingly upset. A hardworking high school student, I had very few days to call my own, and yet I had given up my precious Sundays to help build something that I would be able to enjoy for only a few more years.

I knew I had to tell my father eventually, so I tried to play it cool. "Dad, what would you do if you had been given a ticket to see the 49ers?"

"I'd go." (Leave it to him to be completely logical!)

"But what if that ticket was for this Sunday's game and I already promised Mr. Lee I'd be there?"

"Well, I'd call him and tell him I've got a ticket to the game and can't make it. But I'd be sure to call him—he's expecting you."

"If he's expecting me, he's probably not expecting too much from me. I'm just the gravel mover."

My dad, paying more attention to his newspaper than to me, added, "Remember what the preacher said a while ago—about how the body is made up of different parts? Well, maybe you're not an eye or a nose— maybe you're just a hand."

"No, I don't even qualify as a hand. If anything, I'm just a pinky on the hand."

My father glanced up from his paper and said, "I guarantee you'd miss your pinky if something happened to it."

"Thanks, Dad," I said, but inside my thoughts were more sarcastic and cutting. *Yeah, thanks a lot!*

But he was right. I needed to phone Mr. Lee. Certainly even he would understand that one doesn't win life's lottery very often, and I had just hit the jackpot. I searched for his number, picked up the phone, and then immediately slammed the receiver onto the hook. "I'll call tomorrow."

When tomorrow became today, I went through the very same ritual. I found Mr. Lee's number, picked up the phone, and then slammed the receiver down. "There's still time," I said quietly to myself. "I'll call tomorrow."

The week flew by rapidly, and still I hadn't contacted Mr. Lee. On Saturday I saw him at church. He had made an impassioned appeal for everyone to come and help. I slouched in my pew and stared at my pinky.

When I bumped into him in the church foyer, he said, "I'll see you bright and early tomorrow—right, Mike?"

I felt as if everyone had stopped talking in the foyer and was staring at me, waiting eagerly for my reply. Swallowing hard, I mumbled, "You can count on me."

Figuring that I had just sealed my fate, I called Joel that evening to tell him I couldn't make the game. But when he got on the other end, I couldn't get a word in. "Mike, this is going to be the coolest game," he raced on. "I bought some sodas for the trip there and back, and I even have a new 49er sweatshirt."

I didn't have the heart to back out. "Joel," I said, with dampened enthusiasm, "I can hardly wait."

All night I could feel sweat beading up on the back of my legs. (It's a peculiar tick of mine when I get stressed!) I didn't know what to do. I wanted desperately to go to the game, but I also felt as if something bad might happen to me if I turned my back on my own congregation. Perhaps lightning would strike. Maybe I'd get my hand caught in a door and I'd lose my pinky.

By sunrise I had a plan. Once again I found Mr. Lee's phone number and dialed it. This time I waited until he answered.

"Mr. Lee?"

"Mike. May I help you with something?"

"Well, kind of. It turns out that a friend of mine and I have an important assignment we've got to complete. We've kind of fumbled on the project thus far, and I'm just afraid if we don't huddle together and draw up a play, we might drop the ball." I reasoned that by flinging a few football metaphors at him, my prevarications might not be lies after all. Rather, they were cryptically spoken truths.

"OK, Mike," he said, sounding more disappointed than I would have guessed he would. "School should come first."

I didn't remember saying anything about school, so was it my fault that he misconstrued my clear and obvious statement?

Before my dad took off to work at the gym, he asked, "Hey, did you ever tell Mr. Lee you weren't going to make it?"

"Yeah, Dad! I told him I had another engagement."

My dad grimaced a bit, but figured that while I hadn't been totally honest, I had at least been polite enough to call.

The game itself was surprisingly dull. First, our so-called 50-yard-line tickets were in the top deck section looking down on the end zone. In the distance we could see what appeared to be the 50-yard line, so maybe that's what the seller meant. And while the 49ers won easily, after about the second quarter we got tired of watching Joe Montana fling balls for touchdowns. Plus, it was painfully clear to me that, unlike baseball, football was made to be watched on TV. I missed the play-by-play, missed John Madden's color commentary, missed the instant replays, missed the quirky halftime show, and missed even the commercials. By mid-third quarter the backup quarterback had been thrown in simply because the game had long been decided. It turned out that the highlight of the game was a man who tossed Frisbees onto the field so that his dog could snag them midair. The cheers for the acrobatic dog rivaled the ovations during the game.

Tired of watching dull football and Frisbee-catching dogs, I told Joel that I wanted some nachos and then worked my way out of our row and into the concessions line. Just then I heard a familiar voice. "Mike, imagine seeing you here!"

There in the line across from me stood Joseph, a former student at our school and an occasional visitor at our church. He was two grades ahead of Joel and me, but he had always been friendly to us, despite our obvious disadvantage in age.

"Hey, Joseph. So it's a small world after all." I thought about bursting into the song, but the fat man holding two beers in front of me might not have approved. (Or worse, he might have sung along.) I was genuinely surprised to see Joseph, though pleasantly so.

"Yeah, I'm actually here alone. Great game, huh?"

"For the first quarter, maybe." We both laughed, and then I added, "Hey, Joel is with me, and we're going to pick up some food after the game. Want to join us?"

"You got it. Just meet me here after the crowds thin out."

After the game ended—officially, that is—and what remained of the crowd drifted away, Joseph, Joel, and I went out for sandwiches. All in all, it was a fun day. Not as exciting as I had hoped, but it was better than shoveling gravel or fixing a gymnasium roof.

When I got home, however, I wasn't so sure. Maybe fixing the roof would have been more fun. My dad disliked the work bees as much as I did—he just rarely admitted it—but he said this particular day had been great fun. The women of the church had prepared an elaborate feast for the workers, and the meal was as fun as Family Fun Night. With so many willing helpers, the day went quickly. The guys on the roof laughed at each other's dry humor, which disappointed me, because I love dry humor. I wouldn't have believed that it had actually happened, except for the fact that my dad's a lousy liar. He obviously was telling the truth. "It really felt like we were a family up there. I'm glad I could help out."

Isn't it just my luck that I should miss the best of all work bees for a tiresome football game that was hardly visible from our bird's-eye view? I thought to myself.

I've never been one who thinks church members must give up their private lives so they can be involved in every church activity, every church committee, or every church work bee. But again and again the church has helped me to grow, and every once in a while I have an opportunity to aid the church in turn. As John F. Kennedy really meant to say: "Ask not what your church can do for you, but what you can do for your church." Unfortunately, there is a little-known rule of life that's as bothersome and as inevitable as Murphy's Law—maybe it's one of its corollaries. Simply put, whenever someone schedules a work bee, there will usually be something else more pressing to do. More to the point, if work needs to be done at the church, there will always be something more *interesting* to do.

So why get involved? Why not go to the 49ers game? Won't someone else be there to pick up the slack?

After the letdown of the game, I sat in my room and thought about what my dad had said about the body. Pulling out my trusty concordance, I found the actual passage in 1 Corinthians 12. More than a few times Paul describes the church family by using the metaphor of the body, but I like this one best: "Now the body is not made up of one part but of many. If the foot should say, 'Because I am not a hand, I do not belong to the body,' it would not for that reason cease to be part of the body. And if the ear should say, 'Because I am not an eye, I do not belong to the body,' it would not for that reason cease to be part of the body. . . . But in fact God has arranged the parts in the body, every one of them, just as he wanted them to be" (verses 14–18).

It's an apt metaphor. But as I sat on my bed and thought about the work bee, I began to paraphrase the text a bit: "If the one who can only shovel gravel were to say, 'Because I can't hammer plasterboard, I'm not a part of the body,' he would not for that reason cease to be part of the body. And if the one who should have been there to help finish the roof decided to go to the 49er game, he would not for that reason cease to be part of the body—but he might miss out on an awesome blessing!"

According to Paul, I hadn't stopped being a part of the body, but I sure hadn't been a very productive limb. Unfortunately, Mr. Lee needed a hand—or at least a pinky on the hand—but the hand was sitting in a lousy seat in the nosebleed section of Candlestick Park.

I'd come to understand a little better that being a part of a body sometimes means doing things I don't enjoy—like shoveling gravel. I had learned that there is nothing as beautiful as a body that works in perfect unison—and I mean that both literally and metaphorically. And I was beginning to realize that although my contribution was small, it still mattered—to me as much as to the church. From now on, I determined, I would be a dependable limb of the body, even if I was only a gravel-moving pinky!

The next Saturday I stood in the foyer of our church and talked with some friends. Mr. Lee saw me and said, "Sure could have used an extra hand last Sunday."

"I think you mean an extra pinky," I replied, although I don't think he understood.

I blame what happened next on that infuriating statement, "Be sure your sins will find you out." As I made small talk with Mr. Lee, expressing my apologies for missing the work bee, in walked Joseph. He came so rarely to church that I hadn't anticipated his showing up that week. And wouldn't you know it, Joseph, in his typically loud and sanguine manner, marched right up to me, slapped me on the shoulder, and said, "Wasn't last Sunday great? If you like, I might be able to get more 49ers tickets."

I looked at Mr. Lee and smiled. What else could I do? Fall on my knees, grab his ankles, and grovel? Not knowing what to say, I simply said, "Yep, there's nothing more painful than having your pinky sitting in a football stadium while the rest of the body is somewhere else. I'm so sorry, but from now on I promise to be a loyal pinky."

Mr. Lee looked at me as if I'd lost my mind, as if I were speaking gibberish. But then he seemed to get it. At least I hope he did, because otherwise he probably still thinks I'm a bit wacky. "Now that this monster job is about done, maybe I can catch up with the 49ers myself," he said

"Are you a Niners fan?" I asked.

"Since the Kezar Stadium days." He smiled and began talking with other members. I felt a little better, though I managed to punch Joseph in the arm. (A friendly punch, of course.)

That school year most of my classes took place on the top floor of the new gym. We'd been using it for classes for a couple of years, but at last the entire building was finished. The carpets were new, the brick walls looked smooth, and the new-building smells permeated everything. Not even the aroma of gym socks in the men's locker room could spoil that new-building smell. I felt proud for having helped to build it. Sometimes I'd look out the window and say, "You see that mound of gravel over there by the dumpster? You can thank me for that." But people would merely shrug, demonstrating their ignorance. No one seemed to appreciate my contribution. But then again, we often take our pinkies for granted.

One morning in mid-January the sky unloaded bucketfuls of water on us. It rained so hard that rivers formed fat grooves in the new asphalt parking lot. The sound of rain against our new roof was like waves pounding the beach.

There, in that beautiful new building, I slaved over a tough algebra equation. Hardly noticing the tempest outside, I desperately worked out my calculations. Suddenly I felt a trickle on my head. At first I looked around to see if someone had spit on me, but another cold drop immediately hit my head.

Glancing up, I saw a tiny bulge in the ceiling, like a pimple ready to be popped. As I stared at the pimple, a third drop of water tumbled down and splashed me between the eyes.

Under my breath I muttered, "It's only fitting that the building's first leak should fall on me. I guess I had it coming."

10

Am I a Bad Guy if Some Church Members Really Bug Me?

I'VE SEARCHED THE SCRIPTURES looking for an answer to this one. Although I've been schooled on the golden rule and about loving one's enemies, nowhere in all the Bible have I found a text that reads: "Thou shalt not get annoyed at fellow churchgoers—especially those who are genuinely annoying." The reason for my desperate search for an answer to the tormenting question "Am I a bad guy if some members bug me?" is that some church members do bug me. I mean, *really* bug me.

As you can imagine, I walk a fine line even writing about this, because most of the people who drive me crazy are still alive, and nearly all of them still annoy me. The possibility exists that I bother more than a few myself as well, but I try not to entertain that idea. After all, who couldn't love a cuddly teddy bear like me?

Maybe the Bible says so little about being bothered by fellow believers because it's only a matter of time before it happens. Let's not forget that Peter and Paul didn't always get along. Nor did Paul and John Mark. For that matter, neither did most of the disciples. It's inevitable when diverse people come together that someone will bug someone else. When people of various backgrounds, social standings, political affiliations, parenting styles, or manners meet as one body for one purpose, a beautiful thing can happen: Spirit-made unity. But something else can occur as well: absolute and complete aggravation.

Not to sound grumpy or anything, but I have whole groups of people who frustrate me. I bear my soul somewhat dangerously here, knowing that many readers likely belong to one or more of these groups. But take solace in this: I am likely as annoying to these groups as they are to me, and God has seen fit to bring us together. And He has a reason for this that I'm only now beginning to grasp.

Perhaps the best way to identify some of these exasperating groups of church members is to introduce Mr. Wes Jayson. Mr. Jayson was extraordinary in many ways. He was intelligent, thought-provoking, active, and generous. His wife was an attractive older woman who had probably been movie-star gorgeous in her 20s or 30s. His grandchildren who came to stay with him every summer had more energy than human beings should be allowed to possess, but the Jaysons channeled that energy into constructive activities.

Mr. Jayson may sound like a model church member, and in many ways he was—except for the fact that he bothered me to no end. He was the only person—and thus far remains the only individual—who belonged to every one of my top-four most-annoying groups.

First of all, Mr. Jayson was a member of that ever-exasperating group, the "Bless Their Hearts Club."

Few groups drive me more batty than the Bless Their Hearts Club, a.k.a. the gossipers. As sure as every church service has an offering call, every congregation has at least two gossipers within its midst. I say *two*, because there can be no such thing as one gossiper. Gossip requires both a speaker and a listener. It's the classic If a tree falls and no one hears it does it make a sound? argument. If there's only a gossip *speaker*—a disseminator of steamy tidbits —but no gossip *listener,* then the falling tree isn't making any noise. (Is anyone following my obtuse logic?)

Granted, the church has always frowned on gossip, but we, in our genius, have developed an approach to it that avoids the frowned-upon aspects of it. It's brilliant, really—a means to inoculate one's self from being accused of gossiping. All one must do is preface any gossip with the neat phrase "bless his heart" or "bless her heart" or "bless their hearts." For example, Mr. Jayson would never say, "Of course, you didn't hear this from me, but I understand that the Daleys' marriage is on the rocks." Even the most curious listener would see the red flags flying at the rumble of approaching gossip. However, Mr. Jayson was too quick-minded to make such an error. Instead, he might say, "You know the Daleys, *bless their hearts*—I am very concerned about the state of their marriage. I wonder if there's anything we can do?"

Ah, it's like magic. Suddenly, with only the slightest turn of phrase, Mr. Jayson had refashioned himself from a blatant gossiper into a concerned brother in Christ. And it goes without saying that such semantic maneuvers—and those good at it—really bother me.

By that I do not mean to say that some members of the Bless Their Hearts Club aren't genuine in their concerns. A small few, such as Mr. Jayson, rarely, if ever, exhibited animosity toward anyone, and he, in particular, would go out of his way to help anyone in need. But let's not allow facts to spoil my opinions of him.

If Mr. Jayson belonged only to the Bless Their Hearts Club, I might find him tolerable, even likable. But he was also an active member of the "Martha Club."

Like the Bless Their Hearts Club, the Martha Club exists in every church. Its members are busybodies who generally have the best intentions in mind, which is why they are so oppressive to the rest of us. If a potluck demands one entrée per family, someone from the Martha Club brings three—plus chips and dip and a dessert. If a work bee's in order, a Martha Club member's name appears at the top of the sign-up sheet. No doubt the Martha Club members probably engage in other irritating activities as well, such as balancing their checkbooks, alphabetizing their CDs and DVDs, and organizing their home library according to the Dewey Decimal System, but I can't prove that.

One noticeable trait of the Martha Club is that all of its members seem to be good collectors. If labels need to be gathered from canned goods for a good cause, they tend to raid the grocery store for every participating can. Should the church recycle, the Martha Club members manage to fill fat garbage sacks with cans from the shoulders of the freeway. If the congregation needs to collect clothing for the poor, they manage to have enough in their closets to bring in good articles, not just the junk rags that not even a homeless man in a Manhattan winter would wear.

I don't doubt their intentions, other than their obvious inclination to make the rest of us look bad. Somehow we *must* make those people realize that we don't all have the time or the talent to fix entrées, to remove labels from cans, or to amass plastic soda bottles. Some of us work for a living and need time to watch TV.

Mr. Jayson and his wife always brought two or three entrées to the potluck. Then he would chuckle and say, "Well, the problem was, I couldn't make up my mind what to make." (See? If that's not annoying, I don't know what is.) The pastor often would announce, "I'd like to have Wes Jayson stand up. Do you know how many labels he brought in this month?"

And just to needle me further, he held five posts at the church. First, he was the head librarian. He got that position because he had donated gobs of his own books to the church, and he loved to read. (Members who couldn't afford the latest Christian book could check it out from our church, which was a great idea, except that it was so Martha Club.) Mr. Jayson also taught an adult Sabbath school class; he was a member of the church board *and* the school board; and he was even the chair of the church's social committee. Count it up: that's five posts. I held one: I was a member of the nominating committee to nominate the nominating committee.

The annoyance didn't end there. Along with active membership in both the Bless Their Hearts Club and the Martha Club, Mr. Jayson was rich. Ours was a wealthy town, so we had a number of affluent members. One might call them the "Needle's-Eye Club," because those of us who were poor often quoted Jesus' famous truism "It is easier for a camel to go through the eye of a needle than for a rich man to enter the kingdom of God" (Matthew 19:24). We uttered that text because it made us feel good, maybe even superior. And it helped us to feel less annoyed that Mr. Jayson—and others of his exasperating ilk—were rich, and we were not.

Not that Mr. Jayson flaunted his wealth, and not that he was miserly. To the contrary, the church always remained in the black, and most knew that it was partially because of Mr. Jayson's generosity. I chalked it up as mere exhibition. He drove a plain-Jane Buick, though it was always the newest model. He never dressed rich, but I figured he just lacked fashion sense. I was poor, and even I looked richer than he did, which only infuriated me more.

Last—and this was the proverbial straw for me—Mr. Jayson often griped about our school. Slightly more conservative than the school's principal, Mr. Jayson believed the standards should be stricter. He felt that it should challenge the students academically if they were to go on to good colleges and universities. Furthermore, he believed that there was a wee bit too much fraternizing between the sexes, meaning he disapproved of coed physical education.

An upper-class student at the time, I loved our school. Granted, I had gripes too about my school, though different from Mr. Jayson's. Many of us whined about leaks in the roof (oops!) and worn-out textbooks. However, a school is like one's family: It's OK for those on the inside to fuss about it, but for someone on the outside to make derogatory comments is begging for a fight.

Indeed, Mr. Jayson belonged to the fourth annoying group of church members: "The Meddlers." There always exist those who can't understand one simple maxim about church (or church schools): Things are the way they are because that's the way they are, and even though there may be dozens of better ways of doing something, change is out of the question.

I haven't listed all the annoying groups found within the church, only those four that specifically annoy me. Conveniently I've left out that grating faction that sits around and writes books about annoying groups within the church. (No doubt we'd be better off without them!)

I'm not sure which of all of Mr. Jayson's group memberships caused the problem, but the tide eventually turned against him. Apparently he had bothered others. Maybe they found his "bless their hearts" comments to be trying. Perhaps his workaholic approach to personal ministries intimidated people. Some may have felt that although it may be easier for a camel to enter the eye of a needle than for a rich man to enter the kingdom of heaven, it would be better to seal off the needle's eye just in case. Or most likely, church members didn't appreciate his criticisms of the church school.

For whatever reason, Mr. Jayson had crossed a line and had become an irritant to more than just me. That's when a strange series of events took place.

Rumors began to spread about Mr. Jayson, which seemed to emanate from the Bless Their Hearts Club. Throughout our church, members spoke in hushed voices, saying, "Now, I don't know all the details, but it appears that Wes Jayson, *bless his heart,* was seen last week leaving a bar with another woman." As the rumor spread, Mr. Jayson's heart must have grown into a highly potent organ, considering how many blessings it had received.

For some reason, the rumor made Mr. Jayson more vulnerable to attack, and other complaints began to surface. Members started griping, including those in the Martha Club, that Mr. Jayson did seem to hold an excessive number of church positions. What's more, if the rumor proved true, certainly those responsibilities should be taken from him. A few rather cautious members even suggested that he be stripped of his posts right now simply because it would be too difficult to fill them later.

For the first time I began to feel sympathy for Mr. Jayson. No one else seemed as willing or as capable when it came to those posts, so why shouldn't he be active? And what if the rumor about Mr. Jayson, bless his heart, proved untrue? Wouldn't all this talk have been nothing but destructive drivel?

The big blow came when some members—those bothered by the rumor, his multiple posts, his criticism of the school—began to voice their disapproval of his wealth. "I know he gives to the church, but is it right for us to glorify this man because of his money?" they argued. "I don't understand how he became so wealthy," others complained, "but I know he hasn't shared any with me."

I was ready to scream, "Leave the poor man alone!" Then, as I angrily pointed my finger at all these badgering church members, I realized that it was aimed at me. For the very first time I saw Mr. Jayson not as an irritant—like a speck of dust in one's eye—but a real human being with emotions, concerns, and personality. Sure, everything these shallow-minded, nitpicky gripers were saying reflected my sentiments. However, when he became a real person rather than the object of my scorn, I couldn't help feeling for him.

When Mr. Jayson came to church one Saturday, he seemed beaten down, discouraged. I knew he was aware of the rumor, and I wondered if it was true. The look of despondency reminded me of the classic story of when the Bless Their Hearts Club hurled a woman at Jesus' feet and laid on her accusations of adultery. Jesus' response was simple: "If any one of you is without sin, let him be the first to throw a stone at her" (John 8:7). Of course, no one did. Jesus had an uncanny ability to look at an individual—even someone who deserved to be sneered at—and see a real person. He didn't perceive a walking scandal—no! He viewed an individual with anxieties, pain, love, and potential, just like everyone else. It was His ability to glimpse beyond their needs and see a person that made Jesus so loving.

Everything came to a head for Mr. Jayson at a Thursday night church board meeting. Usually he arrived armed with a variety of issues to raise, mostly about the school. That evening, though, he looked nervous, even shaken. After a brief worship talk about forgiveness and mercy (I think he should have talked about the woman caught in adultery), the pastor announced that an issue needed to come to the attention of the board because it could not be settled privately. Everyone looked at each other in amazement, except for Mr. Jayson.

What had been a mere rumor had become a concrete accusation. Some women in the church stepped forward as witnesses to Mr. Jayson's alleged infidelities. With their own eyes they had seen the so-called smoking gun—Mr. Jayson exiting a bar with a mystery woman.

The room was silent, until our pastor asked, "Mr. Jayson, would you be willing to offer your side of the story?"

We wondered what he might say, considering how incriminating the eyewitness accounts were. How could he possibly wiggle out of this one?

Mr. Jayson rose from his chair and looked at everyone. I remembered how annoying he had been to me, but for the first time I began to wonder if I was the real problem. He seemed so real to me at this moment. The man was flesh and blood, not an abstract nuisance.

"I'm a businessman," he began. "I work with dozens of other businesspeople in order to help them to establish their businesses, to save their businesses, or to strengthen their businesses. I received a call from one of my longtime clients who was in financial trouble. She asked me to meet her at the, uh, so-called bar—which is also a wonderful restaurant. Yes, we were in the bar, but only because the main restaurant was full, and the host informed us that the only tables left were in the bar. We agreed to sit there. And that woman you saw me with is a clothing store owner from downtown, and I am trying very hard to help her salvage her business."

Perhaps there is some irony in having Mr. Jayson hog-tied by gossip, especially gossip dressed up as Christian concern, I thought to myself. Or maybe the irony was in my reaction, wanting so badly to defend a man who had been mistreated because he happened to be zealously active in the church, or because he was rich, or because he had leveled some concerns about our school.

After making a brief statement, Mr. Jayson left the room at the request of the board. The board was then supposed to debate whether or not he could keep his many positions at the church. But before the debate could go anywhere, one board member said, "I move that we absolve Wes of any wrongdoing. It seems clear that this is all a misunderstanding, and Wes, bless his heart, has suffered enough." (At last someone used that phrase— "bless his heart"—in an appropriate manner!)

Fortunately, the entire board was sympathetic with Mr. Jayson's explanation—even those who had little sympathy for Mr. Jayson. Most of the board members were businesspeople, so they could relate to his story. They voted unanimously that there should not even be a debate, and he was exonerated. The weird part is that I was ecstatic for him.

A few days later at church, one of our wiser and older elders offered prayer. Unlike most of his prayers, this one was short and pithy. In a quivering voice he said, "Father, forgive us, for we have not loved as we should. Amen."

That was it? At first I assumed he hadn't prepared. Maybe he couldn't find his lengthy list of requests in his suit jacket. Or perhaps he was getting old and had lost his train of thought.

Or could he have prayed the right prayer at the right moment?

I felt a horrible sense of guilt. So many people in the church drove me crazy. But did I love them as I should? No! Was I ready to throw a first stone—or at least join in after someone else had started the flinging? Absolutely. "Father, forgive me, for I have not loved as I should," I whispered.

I confess that I still get annoyed by people in the church. Mr. Jayson continued to upset me even after his absolution, though I was *learning*—emphasis on the word learning—to love him anyway. (Apparently I *did* learn, because there are few people I admire more in the church today than him, and it is the very traits that once bugged me most about him that make him so commendable.) The turning point for me came at the appalling realization that occasionally people bugged Jesus as well. The Pharisees, the Sadducees, the priests, and the scribes frustrated Him. Sometimes He leveled harsh accusations at them—just read Matthew 23 to get a taste. He also got more than a little perturbed at the money changers. Jesus even was so rude as to turn their tables over, grab a whip, and kick them out of church. Imagine what a stir such a person would cause today.

To be honest, those stories encourage me. They tell me that Jesus was not so different from me in some respects. And hey, I never felt the urge to knock over Mr. Jayson's table or chase him out of church with a whip. OK, so I didn't share it that often.

But Jesus was different from me in one very important detail: despite getting annoyed at people, He never stopped loving them. The only way He could do that was by seeing them as human beings.

What Would Happen if the Pastor Left His Lapel Mike On?

I'VE TOUCHED ON THE deeply reflective subjects thus far—the essential stuff, such as church boredom, game-night fights, and annoying church members. Yet at times it's important to ask the lesser questions—those that have little importance, even less relevance, and probably no consequence whatsoever. Yet despite their seeming inconsequentiality, they still remain unanswered, and I feel it my God-given duty to respond to them, in part because I know the answers.

Take, for example, the pressing question: What would happen if the pastor accidentally left his lapel mike on after he or she had left the platform?

Believe it or not, I experienced the answer to this one.

During my short stint as a pastor, I enjoyed nothing so much as preaching. Our church was tiny (about 40 members), and we rented a church building from a large Disciples of Christ congregation of about 400. Needless to say, we didn't fill the seats. Even if we had managed 100 people (and we never once did), the sanctuary would have looked sparse.

We kept meeting in the large building because we believed that it demonstrated our faith. After all, if we relocated to a structure that fit us, we'd be denying the ability to grow (not unlike my logic when shopping for pants).

Still, we had ways to make the church seem less empty. For one, we encouraged everyone to sit toward the front. Of course, no one occupied the front row, because front rows in church were long ago deemed off-limits. There's no rational explanation for the aversion to the front row, but maybe it goes back to people's high school days when the cool crowd congregated in the back row. Only nerds (like me) sat in the front row, and nothing, I guess, could be more nerdlike than a church nerd. Alas, we had no church nerds.

The other tack I took to help minimalize the feeling of being a scattered few was to use the lapel mike.

When I preached, I enjoyed moving around, and a pulpit was too confining, like trying to do aerobics in tight jeans. The lapel mike, neatly clipped to my tie—or my shirt when I didn't wear a tie (was I a fashion rebel, or what?)—freed me to move not only my legs but also my hands. At times I'm convinced that my mouth cannot function without my hands, which may indicate some faulty wiring in my brain. However, as a storyteller, I liked having my hands free.

Fortunately, our church was blessed with an extremely conscientious sound person. His name was Wolfgang. Every Saturday morning he diligently arrived early to make sure every microphone was positioned correctly on the appropriate microphone stand. He tested the CD player to see if the EQ was set just right, so that there weren't too many booming low frequencies and too many clangy high frequencies. Most important, he checked the batteries in my lapel mike.

At first I didn't want to use the device. "Wolfgang, couldn't I just hold a microphone?" I protested. "Maybe a wireless hand-held microphone would be even better."

But Wolfgang would have nothing of that. "All the good preachers I know use lapel microphones." I tried to parse those words. Was he complimenting me, calling me a good preacher who lacked only a lapel mike? Or was he attempting to rescue my preaching through the use of the apparatus? I didn't want to know, but I tried to assume the better of the two options.

I tried the mike and liked it. Before I had come to the congregation, someone had had the foresight to purchase a superior microphone, and I began to enjoy the freedom it gave me.

When Wolfgang handed me the mike, he gave me the same speech, as if he'd forgotten that I had long since memorized his admonition. "Remember to turn the mike on before you speak. You'll know it's not on if you speak and you can't hear your voice." (I can only guess that he was convinced that I was an idiot.) "And most importantly, remember to turn it off when you're done. Sometimes I'm not at the board to shut it down, so you might say something you'll, uh, regret."

First, I reasoned, I would never say anything I regret. Second, I would never forget to turn the device off. Sadly, I was wrong on both accounts.

For those who have never preached before, let me explain a few things. Though most pastors won't admit it, they experience a reaction of satisfaction when a sermon goes well. One can feel it when it's happening, as when a pitcher senses when their good curve ball is working. It has little or nothing to do with the effectiveness of the sermon itself, because that is the Holy Spirit's work. I have preached a sermon that would have given my homiletics professor (a snooty way of saying my "preaching teacher") posttraumatic stress syndrome, only to see the Holy Spirit use my dreadful talk to change a life.

Still, let me say what most pastors will not. When a sermon is working—that is, when the substance is wrapped in passion and fused with sizzling articulation, delivery, and word choice—one almost wants to celebrate, to pump one's fist, to pat one's back, but that would be bigheaded (not to mention ill-mannered).

One Sabbath morning I was on my game. I knew it almost as soon as I woke up. There was just something about the morning: I had replaced the blades on my razor so that my shave was smooth and clean; Michelle had made pancakes with real maple syrup; and I found my keys after searching for less than 10 minutes. When I arrived at the church, I found everything in place, which was a rarity indeed. The names in the bulletin were even spelled correctly, which was a first. Absolutely everything about this particular morning was right.

I had prepared a sizzling whizbanger of a sermon about approaching God with humility, though not because my congregation was particularly arrogant. Sometimes a sermon topic comes to mind simply because it's what the preacher needs to hear, and the congregation will hopefully benefit as well.

I used as my primary text Matthew 23:12, taken from one of Jesus' few hellfire-and-brimstone sermons. As He spoke to a large crowd He leaped into a righteous outburst against the Pharisees, comparing them to snakes and mausoleums and blind tour guides. At the heart of His harsh critique Jesus declared, "For whoever exalts himself will be humbled, and whoever humbles himself will be exalted."

I couldn't have said it better myself. Nor was there anything I could have said to augment Jesus' words. But I was a preacher, which means that in spite of the clarity of His words, in spite of the fact that Jesus—especially in this instance—needed little explanation, I couldn't help expounding.

"It's a simple formula that's one part promise, one part conditional prophecy," I declared. "If you want to be exalted, be humble. Of course, if you want to be exalted, then you are not being humble, which means you will, in the end, be humbled. And if you are humble, then you will be exalted, which is not the same as being humbled, which is a condition of humiliation that doesn't necessarily lead to being humble, a state of mind that Jesus promises will result in one's being exalted. Is anyone getting this?"

The people said, "Amen."

Of course, I had no idea what I had just said, but it sure felt good on the tongue, and it must have been deep, because not even I fully understood the layers of meaning in that multidimensional sermon. When the sermon ended, I felt great.

Having admitted at the start that I would forget to turn off my lapel mike, it probably goes without saying that I forgot to turn it off. I've heard the horror stories about pastors then going straight to the restroom while the amused congregation listened in—and I know of at least one such account that is true. But if I had done that, it would have proved merely entertaining. What I did, instead, was horrifying.

I stepped into the side hallway that led back to the foyer. At our church I would slip out the side in order to get to the foyer and greet people as they left the sanctuary. Feeling so good about my sermon as I walked toward the foyer, I pumped my fist and said, "Billy Graham, eat your heart out!"

When I reached the foyer, Wolfgang was there to meet me. I thought that was strange, because he never waited for me in the back. *Maybe,* I thought to myself, *he wants to congratulate me on my stupendous little discourse. Or perhaps he's going to tell me how glad he is to have recorded the sermon, because it was one for the ages.*

But no, his eyes were large like two moons hovering just above the horizon. Strangely, he didn't say anything, though his lips were apart about one inch. Glancing down at his hand, I saw his finger pointing—straight at my lapel mike.

"I would have turned it off," he explained as I switched it off, "but I had to use the restroom. Unfortunately, I was piping the sound through the speakers in the restroom ceiling, so I heard everything, and so did the congregation."

Not to change subject or anything, but I remember as a fourth-grade boy having a seventh grader punch me in the belly out on the playground. I don't remember why he did it, though I'm sure it was entirely his fault. (When you're a fourth grader, it's always the seventh grader's fault!) But I sure remember the blow. The pain was excruciating, wringing out any oxygen left in my body. I strained for a breath, but couldn't find one. That horrible, painful, panicky feeling I had experienced on the playground returned to me there in the church foyer.

In that moment of horror I had an argument with myself: Should I hide so I didn't have to greet every member as he or she walked out, or should I stand there and pray that no one understood me? Maybe they thought I said, "Billy Graham, speak your part out." Or maybe "Billy Graham, leave your doubt out." Or even "Silly ham, eat your lard out."

I elected to stand at the door, greet members, and take my medicine.

There are advantages to having a church with a sense of humor—an all-too-rare and precious quality among parishioners. I heard comments such as "Thanks, Pastor Billy, uh, I mean Mike." One woman, a wise mother of four, said, "Thank you, Pastor, for giving me the best sermon illustration I have ever heard." (*Great,* I thought. I had handed her an object lesson that she could use on her children the rest of their lives. At a loss for words, I simply said, "Glad I could be used of God.")

I drove home feeling about as humbled as I had ever been. Pulling out of the nearly empty parking lot, I talked out loud to God. "OK, God, I think You just proved that there is truth in that text. I exalted myself and, needless to say, I have been humbled. I prefer the word 'humiliated.' Or how about 'horrified'? 'Mortified'? Or just plain 'embarrassed'?"

As I turned onto the main street of the town I replayed the morning's incident in my head. Then I said, "Help me out, God. Give me something I can take home that will make me feel better." (I have this annoying habit of talking to God in the car. I hope He doesn't mind, although other drivers maybe should.)

Just before the on-ramp onto the freeway I saw a tiny church building that was probably too small for even our microscopic congregation. It looked a bit run-down, but it had a sign on its front lawn. It said: "The first test of a great man is humility."

"Yeah, thanks, God!" I said in a mock-sarcastic voice. "That's just what I needed to read. Maybe those words will help me sleep better tonight."

Don't ask me why, but as I thought about the words and the sheer irony that they'd be there at all, I started to laugh. It started as a breathy, sputtering chuckle, like an AMC Pacer on a cold morning, but soon the laughter revved into a muffler-free roar. Tears blurred my vision, and I tried to see the road. (Fortunately, no cops were patrolling anywhere nearby, or I might have had to step out of the car and walk the yellow line.)

When I gained my composure, I said, "OK, You win, God. I still feel pretty humbled, but considering how hard You're trying to teach me a lesson, I at least don't feel like dirt."

So what, one may ask, would happen if a pastor left his lapel mike on? I can't answer that universally, but there is a good chance he might learn a valuable lesson—that whoever humbles himself will be exalted, and whoever exalts himself had better hope the sound person doesn't have to use the restroom.

Do I Have to Hear That Music Again?

I PLAY A GUITAR. If I really want to, I can do it extremely loud, and sometimes I really, really want to. Also I enjoy a pounding drum, a throbbing bass guitar, a whiny keyboard—everything that was once taboo in the church, and in many, many circles still is.

To make matters worse, I have long hair and a beard—sometimes even a goatee! My guitar is painted in psychedelic colors as if it were straight out of the Haight-Ashbury days. Everything about me seems to disqualify me from contributing to the great debate about music in the church.

And yet most people who don't know me (and some who do) would be surprised at how eclectic and diverse my musical tastes are. I have little patience for those who subscribe to the "one-genre God theory"—that is, that God likes just one style of music, and it happens to be theirs.

I've heard it said that God enjoys classical music, which may be true. What's not to like about Western Europeans pouring their genius into gaudy and, at times, garish uses of horsehair, catgut, and eucalyptus wood. I love the classics, although I'm especially partial to opera and operatic singing. (I have some operatic training, but about the only thing that's operatic about me today is my waistline.)

More than a few have claimed that God's a closet bluegrass fan. Could be, considering the fact that bluegrass is the music of mountain people—the kind of common masses that Jesus hung out with when He walked the earth. And who's to say that a little American twang with a hearty Irish influence doesn't warm His heart?

Also people have told me that the music of "church" is gospel music, and that may well be true too. Who's to say that God isn't partial to the rhythms, harmonies, and movements that have their roots in a rich and ancient African culture? I can't imagine that God would focus on the music of Europe and North America without turning an interested ear to an entire continent's worth of brilliant music.

Or what about the Latin rhythms? If there is one place God is adored, it is Latin America. So might one make the case that the rhythms of that region—even as they spill into our popular culture—may be the style of music that God likes most?

I have a good friend who believes with all his heart that rock and roll is the music God will use to save the world. No doubt it's the most popular music in the world, so why wouldn't God employ it? He's a practical Deity, isn't He? Besides, rock and roll—as with country music and pop— is nothing more than an amalgamation of Europe's and Africa's music stirred in a melting pot called America, and later co-opted by the British. Doesn't such a multicultural approach sound like our multifaceted God?

Or what about a good hymn? Doesn't God love hymns? For sure I do. How can one not like old drinking songs and nationalistic melodies dressed up with spiritual poems? In mainland Europe church musicians began to play the hymns on a newfangled contraption called the "organ," although many Protestants of the early Renaissance believed the garish instrument was evil and preferred their hymns sung a cappella or with guitar. I love a good organ, though I don't mind a cappella singing or the guitar.

The world has so many styles of music, and I've only scratched the surface. So which is the style that God prefers? What should we sing in church? Or maybe the question more often asked is What should we *not* sing in church?

A common answer is Don't sing anything in church that has its origins in "the world." Well, there goes the bathwater *and* the baby. Such a standard may do away with the tub as well. Certainly hymns and classical music are out. No more gospel music or Latin rhythms or even bluegrass. Maybe Gregorian chant might survive that standard, but I'll have to research that one. (Then again, Gregorian chant is a part of the rich Roman Catholic tradition, and the Protestants might feel that a resurgence of chant would indicate a trend toward being, as Garrison Keillor called it, "soft on Catholics.")

I don't have an easy answer, and the ones I have managed to piece together will never satisfy everyone. But I do have six years' experience as a "minister of music" at a small church in Napa, California, that has taught me a few things. And I have three years as a full-time recording artist and performer that has also been informative. It hasn't made me a "know-it-all," but it has helped me to be a "know-a-little," which is better than a "know-nothing."

I signed a contract with a Christian record company when I was about 24 years old. Being young and stupid and starry-eyed, I thought that I'd stumbled upon my "big break." It was the Cinderella moment that most musicians dream about but very rarely get to experience.

The signing itself was almost anticlimactic. We met in a tight booth at a Marie Callender's restaurant, and we toasted my career with an extra serving of potato-cheese soup. And thus was born my professional career— please pass the cornbread!

I had no idea how intense the actual recording process would be, but as we built the tracks for songs I had written, it continually revitalized me. We often worked into the wee hours of the night—2:00 or 3:00 a.m.— and when we'd had enough, I would drive an hour and a half up Highway 80 toward home. Then the next day I'd get up at 6:00 a.m. to commute to the studio and start the whole process again.

Many in my church were excited for me. Some who had regularly encouraged me felt personally vindicated by my apparent success. They'd say such things as "Mike's gonna be a star, and I saw it coming." I doubt they could see it coming, but I liked the part about being a star.

When we were about halfway through the recording project, our church planned a statewide young adult convocation. Our sanctuary was large enough to pack in about 1,500 people, so it seemed the ideal location for a large gathering. The pastors planned to invite young adults—especially postcollege adults who often feel out of place in the church—from across the entire state for a weekend of contemporary music, good preaching, and practical seminars. I thought it was a great idea, in part because I was one of those young adults who wanted to fit into the church but didn't know how. (Somehow we need to figure out a smoother transition between youth and adulthood. As it is now, a twentysomething Christian feels too old for youth group activities but too young to hobnob with older adults.)

The pastoral staff asked if I would sing and play my guitar for the church service—one or maybe two songs. I was honored and thrilled to do so. "Is there anything in particular you'd like for me to play?" I asked them.

The pastor in charge of the weekend's music said, "Oh, just something that will inspire young adults. And make it something contemporary."

Musically speaking, "contemporary" is a relative term, so I was unclear as to what he meant and should have pressed for more information. Our church, in general, was conservative, but not to the point of being medieval. And considering the audience—young adults like me—I decided to play a mellow folk-rock song and a bluesy piece.

The convocation date arrived, and young adults poured in from all over the state. The church was packed, and the worship service would be broadcast live over the radio. That made me more nervous than I already was, but I tried to relax. "Breathe in through your mouth and out through your nose," I told myself. It didn't help.

The time came for me to step onto the platform. I had considered singing with canned backup music, but I thought it would be more appropriate to accompany myself with a guitar. That way the more conservative listeners wouldn't be offended by the bass and drums of the sound tracks, while the less conservative listeners would still appreciate the hip, unplugged feel.

Stepping up to the mike, I started picking a slow folk song. I worried that it was a bit too slow for the audience, but I'm often overly cautious. After that, I launched into the blues.

The blues originated in the Mississippi delta area and came out of the African-American experience of the American South. A widespread myth claims that the blues are an unhappy music. More often the genre is a jubilant sound about real life and the real world. It's a beautiful music, really—that is, when one understands it. Having always admired the blues greats of our American past, I sat down one day to write a gospel blues song. I called it "Multipurpose God."

The song came out of an experience I had had while walking the streets near Fisherman's Wharf in San Francisco. At nearly every corner in the tourist sectors of the city one can find street musicians playing guitars, bongos, or saxophones. It drives my wife, Michelle, crazy that I feel compelled to stop and listen to nearly every one. Maybe it's because I'm a musician that my heart hurts for someone pouring their heart into a song while disinterested passers-by scarcely offer them a glance, let alone a coin.

On this one occasion I heard a talented guitar player who sang a passionate song with a skilled voice. His jeans were ripped, his T-shirt dirty, and his song simple. I can still remember the name of his song: "Get High and Die."

As I listened to his sad, pathetic, but transfixing song, I thought to myself, *Wouldn't it be great to pull out my own guitar and plant myself next to Mr. Get-High-and-Die and sing about a God who can handle anything this world throws at us—a multipurpose God who's a better solution than drugs?* Hence my feeble attempt at composing a blues song.

I launched into my blues song at church. Having sung it 50 times or more in at least 50 other churches, I wasn't overly worried about the song's reception. But I should have been.

When I finished the song, I received a weak but polite applause and sat down. I had no idea the hullabaloo I had just unleashed.

Apparently a torrent of angry phone calls blew into the head pastor's office. The protests came from older people mostly, but some young people, as well, voiced "concern" about the sinister song. The pastor, new to his position, must have felt enormous pressure as more and more influential people from the church board began to gripe. One outspoken board member said, "I will never set foot in this church if Mike Mennard is ever allowed to sing here again."

Ironically, I was oblivious to the commotion. One church member had expressed her disapproval to me, but she was kind about it. "It's not my kind of music," she said, "but I understand you were trying to appeal to the young adults." In my ignorance I assumed that was how most of those who disliked the song would respond.

In retrospect, one of the most fortunate decisions Michelle and I have ever made was to miss church the following week. Instead, we decided to attend a camp meeting about three hours north of us. (We craved both the spiritual retreat and also the massive redwood trees surrounding the camp meeting.) It was a fortunate decision because of what transpired while we were gone.

The pastoral staff had received so many complaints—actually, there were only about a dozen serious ones, but they were vociferous and came from high-ranking members—that they published an apology in the church bulletin. The upside to the apology is that they didn't use my name. The downside is that there was hardly a soul in that church who didn't know to whom it referred. And the *really* downside was that I was still fully unaware of the hue and cry I had unthinkingly caused.

Shortly after we returned from the camp meeting I began to sense that something bad had happened. When I ran into our small-town market to buy some milk a woman I had never met walked up to me and said, "I'm sorry they did that. I don't think there was anything to apologize for." I was so confused by her cryptic comment that I didn't venture to ask what she meant.

By Monday morning, however, I knew. Every friend I had in the church had either called me at home or work or had stopped to talk to me. (There are disadvantages to living in a tiny town of 3,000 people where nearly half of the population attends the same church.)

The elders decided that they would not allow me to play in the church for an indefinite period of time. Since I didn't know about the decision, I just figured everyone had lost his or her nerve to ask me. I felt horrible— like a sudden bout with the stomach flu. The last thing I ever wanted to do was offend anyone.

My recording project, *Grace (and Other Stuff),* came out about four months after the incident, and I began the lonely job of touring. I loved touring, and yet I did much of it by myself or with my dad (who ran my sound equipment) and Michelle. It was draining work—physically and spiritually. I wanted so badly to run to my home church and beg for their prayers, but I was too ashamed even to ask such a thing. Somehow, I felt as if I'd let them down and didn't deserve their prayers. Besides, I figured they wouldn't be interested in praying for the infidel who had offended them, so I never asked. I should have, but I never did. I was on the road most weekends, so I rarely even got to visit my own congregation, but I wondered if that wasn't for the best.

After a year and a half of touring and full-time ministry, I was a different person. No longer the cocky musician with stars in his eyes, I had been humbled. God had done amazing things through my ministry, and I knew that it had to be Him, because it sure wasn't me. It's strange to say that at the peak of my music career (and it was a short-lived peak), I felt more depressed than I'd ever felt before. Lonely and disheartened, I was sure I didn't have a church family anymore. That sense of loss alone was the most devastating blow to me, because the church had always been central to my life.

Then something amazing happened. I received a phone call from the youth pastor asking me to lead the worship singing and to sing for the church service. I felt immediate fear (OK, more like absolute terror) but I said, "You bet I will."

One well-meaning church member had referred to me as "the incarnation of Satan," and I was tired of thinking of myself in that way. (I'm not kidding—someone actually called me that!) But I wanted only to be accepted. So I worked up a simple arrangement of a hymn—one of my favorites, "This Is My Father's World." I'd play it on my guitar so it still sounded post-1960s, but it was a safe selection nonetheless.

More terrified than I had ever been, I walked onto the platform and led the worship songs—preselected by the pastoral staff. Then I performed my hymn arrangement. It would be an understatement to say I put everything I had into it. I wanted it to bring honor to God, yes; but I desperately wanted my church family back, and I thought that if I did a good job (and didn't offend anyone), they'd like me again. (I'm glad that God doesn't work that way, but sometimes we act as if He does.)

As I sang, I felt terrifyingly vulnerable, like the woman who was hurled at the feet of Jesus. As did that adulterous woman, I was just waiting for stones to begin to fly. But when I finished, I heard favorable applause. For a church that generally frowned on applause, it felt like a standing ovation to me. I interpreted it as a warm statement that said, "Welcome back home, Mike."

After church several people shook my hand and thanked me for the song, including some of my more vocal critics. Then I began to hear gripes, but they were a bit different. One member complained, "When I heard you were singing, I made sure my whole family came. But why did you do such a boring song?"

Another member said, "You done good, Mike, but I prefer your more contemporary stuff—not that singing-band music."

I looked at Michelle and commented, "You know, when it comes to music in the church, sometimes you can't win for losing."

That week my wife attended a large committee meeting that included many of the church's elders. It was the first time the committee had met, and its members had yet to get fully acquainted with each other. However, before the session began, one elder said, "I'm so glad that we're allowing Mike Mennard to sing in our church again. I think he was banned long enough."

Tension instantly filled the room. Unfortunately, the well-meaning elder didn't know that the woman sitting next to him was Michelle, but of course everyone else did. It was the first that Michelle or I had heard about an official ban, and when that poor elder realized what had just happened, he was mortified. After the committee meeting he apologized to my wife and said, "I hope I didn't just exceed my bounds and offend you miserably."

"Well, sometimes it helps to heal a wound when the wound can be exposed to air," she replied.

Indeed, I was restored into the good graces of the church, and I couldn't have been happier about it. Both sides had made mistakes, and we freely acknowledged that. But time heals a lot of wounds, and they allowed me to sing now and then. Of course, they always prefaced their requests with a small plea: "Mike, remember your audience." And I always answered, laughing, "Oh, I always do. Believe me, I always do."

Again and again the Psalms implore us to "sing to the Lord a new song." I'm convinced that God must get tired of the old songs, or He wouldn't keep begging for new ones. As a composer, I couldn't be happier with the request. But I'm also aware that worship often succeeds best when accompanied by a certain amount of comfort. Discomfort can be provocative, but it can also be a distraction. And sometimes when I'm worshiping God, I want to do so with my whole mind—and that means no distractions.

The problem is—and this is what six years as a minister of music has taught me—people's comfort levels often have a great deal to do with what they grew up with. In general (and I'm grotesquely overgeneralizing here), those who were young in the 1970s enjoy the praise music that came out of that decade. They find it deeply spiritual, and it meets their needs. One such member said to me, "Those songs remind me why I became a Christian back in my teenage days in the seventies."

Those who were young in the 1950s remember the hymns and the "high church" music still prevalent in the denomination, or maybe even some George Beverly Shea songs. Such songs continue to make their worship experience seem more meaningful, more comfortable, and, yes more spiritual. One such member put it this way: "Those churchy songs just speak to me better."

Today's youth—those fortunate enough to listen to the excellent new worship music being written today—are enjoying a new wave of praise songs that has swept through Christianity, and they wonder why we performed all that "old fogy" music in the first place. Of course, the old fogy music they refer to is the stuff that was brand-new when I was a teenager, so I guess that makes me an old fogy.

One day a sudden realization came to me: People's ideal worship experience sometimes has as much to do with their adolescence as it does with personal tastes or spiritual value. Frequently it's not so much about "appropriateness" or "quality" or even "message" as it is about nostalgia and comfort level—often fixed in stone before we reach full adulthood. But I say this not as a criticism, and I'm not entirely sure there is even anything wrong with this repeatedly observed phenomenon. I'm troubled far less by our gravitation toward a worship comfort level than I am by how we have tried dealing with it.

During the past decade or so, the way we've tackled the problem (if it is, indeed, a problem) has been to splinter our churches, to have different congregations that meet different needs. In larger towns and cities churches have tried to fill a niche by becoming the "contemporary church," the "traditional church," the "gospel church," or even the "praise church." While that seems like an easy fix, it is a sad development, as far as I'm concerned, because one of the beautiful functions of religion is to connect us to something deeper, richer, and yes, *older* than we are. If our worship experience is only as old as we are, it's a shallow one indeed. And yet, another purpose for religion is to worship, and sometimes that means listening to God's desperate appeal for "new songs."

So what should we do?

Again, I don't have *the* answer, and the one I'm about to put forward will not satisfy everyone. But perhaps it will spur thinking.

I'd like to return to the notion that I brought up in chapter 1 of this book—that when it comes to worship, we are not the audience. *God* is. Contrary to what I once believed, God doesn't have a favorite style of music. But He sure loves a genuine song from a contrite heart. Christian music is full of superstars, but I wonder if God doesn't enjoy Local Joe and his musical squeeze-box more than the slick sounds of Nashville or Hollywood—that is, if Joe's heart is real and his praise authentic.

As for me, I'd rather hear a hymn done well then a groovy pop song done poorly—and vice versa. Church music should reflect the makeup of each individual congregation, and members ought to revel in the power of the Spirit to unite us—in spite of variances in musical tastes.

Even the most traditional church would be wise to find an outlet for a young teenager who has been taking guitar lessons. And even the rowdiest praise service should not forget that they are a part of a tradition that is older than they are, and that there's something beautiful, mysterious, and triumphant about connecting with congregations gone by through an old hymn. But when hymns are sung, try telling the stories behind them. Often when people discover why a song was written, it takes on a power that few praise choruses can muster.

And what should the songs portray—whether they be hymns or folk songs or rock songs or chants? Psalm 107:8 says: "Let them give thanks to the Lord for his unfailing love and his wonderful deeds for men." Well, that's a good start: sing songs that document His love and all His feats. Or we can "proclaim your love in the morning and your faithfulness at night," as Psalm 92:2 recommends. And when we sing about these good things— no matter the style—it seems that God likes His music loud. I've looked very hard and have yet to find a single biblical request for quiet communal singing. No, the Bible more often entreats us to "shout to the Lord," and to "sing aloud." (I'm not suggesting we do away with our quiet repertoire of "Day Is Dying in the West" or "Abide With Me," only that we sing them wholeheartedly, never weakly.)

What's more, let the music be done well. I'm a big fan of the word "rehearsal."

After all, if God is the audience, let's offer up our best.

13

Why Is a Backpack Trip Considered a Vacation to Everyone but the Youth Pastor?

ALAS, THE YOUTH PASTOR is the most misunderstood creature on earth—or at least in the church.

To many it appears as if the youth pastor gets paid to have fun. Certainly the ones who survive the youth-pastoring ordeal *are* having fun, because if they're not, they tend to burn out faster than a northern California hillside in late July. And because most youth pastors are fresh out of college—in large part because they're still young enough and naive enough to relate to their target audience—there's an underlying belief that they will one day grow up to be "real" pastors.

In defense of the skeptics, the rampant suspicion of youth pastors among parishioners is understandable. I have shared in their wariness. What else are, we the common churchgoers, to think when we see the youth pastor following his flock of pubescents to the beach, to the water slides, or to the ski slopes? A day's work might involve waterskiing at a nearby lake, hosting a late-night video marathon, or busing a group to see the hot new Christian music group. Granted, they have worship talks to plan, some counseling to confer, and maybe even a few house calls to perform, but all in all the youth pastor's job description sounds cushy. Sure beats being chained to a cubicle from 8:00 to 5:00 every day. And it is better than being a "real" pastor with full-length sermons to write, prayer meetings to plan, and tumultuous board meetings to chair.

But I know only too well that such a view is a gross misconception. I have learned my lesson. And maybe that is what compels me to come to the youth pastor's defense. And since I've never been a youth pastor, I can support them without sounding defensive. Furthermore, no one else seems to feel the need to espouse them, so I gladly take on the burden.

Throughout my formative teenage years I was blessed to have one of the greatest youth pastors on the planet—Pastor Ron. In an age when so many youth grow up and leave the church, it is not coincidence that most of the members of our youth group remain believers still today. Pastor Ron was a friend, a teacher, a mentor, and a cool guy. He was also the meanest—and I mean that in a good way—miniature golf player in our town, which is a plus for a youth pastor. (I recommend that all youth pastors take Minigolf 101 in seminary. It *will* come in handy.)

But apparently God didn't mean for our youth group to horde him, and Pastor Ron accepted an offer to work in Maryland. Although we knew the decision was right, that didn't mean it felt good to us. We staged a terrific "roast" for him as a goodbye party, reminding him of every blunder he might have made. (This is one of the disadvantages to youth pastoring: your congregation is observant enough to see your every flaw and young enough to feel no scruples about pointing them out.) But our intense laughter was followed by equally intense tears as we thanked him for his time, his attention, and his love.

As soon as Pastor Ron moved away, everyone began to feel sorry for his replacement before the individual had even been chosen. Shaking their heads with pity, people said such things as "Well, I sure feel sorry for whoever has to fill his shoes." But our congregation did two things right in picking Pastor Ron's replacement. One, we prayed a lot. I think God had someone in mind for us already, so our prayers did more to unite and focus the pray-ers than it did to persuade God. The second thing we did right, probably thanks to those prayers, is that we didn't pick someone who could fill Pastor Ron's shoes. Instead, we chose someone who brought his own pair.

The new guy's name was Pastor Mike. He was young and handsome, with a beautiful wife and three small children. I confess, however, that the youth group—me included—maintained a wait-and-see attitude at first. We listened to his lower-key worship talks and tried to adjust to his more phlegmatic approach to all youth functions. Although there was little not to like about Pastor Mike, it's hard following a legend. As a result we would not fully embrace him until he had passed the most important test of all—the backpack trip.

(It sounds like we were mean. But we weren't ~~mean~~—we were *youth*. We were young enough to know everything, yet not quite old enough to know that we knew nothing.)

The annual backpack trip had become a summer tradition for our youth group. Pastor Ron always planned it for the end of the summer so it could serve as a shot in the arm for the new year. (For some reason we always regarded the start of school as the beginning of a new year, which may explain why New Year's Eve celebrations rang hollow.)

Though I never would have admitted it then, I never liked backpacking. Maybe I simply didn't like sleeping on hard ground with sharp rocks under me. Perhaps it was the challenge of packing a week's worth of food in a pouch barely big enough to hold a watermelon. (There definitely wasn't room in the pouch for the watermelon after I had stuffed it full of ramen, ramen, and more ramen.) Or most likely it was the calorie-burning exertion that comes with long hikes. After all, I've been saving those calories for when I have to run to the hills during the time of trouble.

To his credit, Pastor Mike immediately recognized the importance of the backpack trip. He knew it was vital not only as a means for the youth group to learn valuable things about themselves and God, but also as an avenue to win the youth themselves to his corner. And I think that because I had worked so closely with Pastor Ron in planning some of the key events in the past, Pastor Mike asked if I would take charge of the backpack trip.

I wanted to say, "That's *your* job. Besides, do you know how much I dislike backpacking? Do I look like Mr. Outdoors? Mr. *Field & Stream?*" Instead I replied, "Pastor Mike, I'd be thrilled to."

I figured that by handing the reins over to me, Pastor Mike was begging for a lifeline to pull him out of the treacherous waters he now found himself in. What I didn't realize then, but do now, is that this was Pastor Mike's modus operandi—pass the baton of responsibility on to the youth themselves so they will learn to be stronger leaders in the future. It didn't mean that he wasn't involved in nearly every decision, but we certainly had the sense that we were making the hard choices.

Before the trip itself, we called a meeting in order to teach the neophytes how to pack a pack, how to pitch a tent, and how to fry potatoes with a tiny cookstove. We tried to explain the basics, such as why it's important to pack more than one pair of underwear. Plus we emphasized that no bathroom facilities existed along the trail, so a small shovel and a roll of toilet paper were a must. Also we outlined the need for insect repellent, good shoes, thick socks, and a mummy bag. Finally we encouraged them to bring their Bibles—not a massive volume that a family might display in the living room to impress its guests, but a lightweight tome, perhaps a paperback New Testament with Psalms and Proverbs.

Everyone nodded their head and seemed to understand, which made me a little nervous. What's more, this year's bunch had no troublemakers, which made me even more concerned. Everything seemed to be falling into place too well.

Pastor Mike then gave me an awesome and terrifying assignment. "Mike, why don't you be the one to speak around the campfire each night. It would be a great experience for you, and I think the younger ones look up to you." I don't know if they admired me, but I did relish the experience.

I decided to go through the entire book of Philippians, which has only five chapters but has gobs of good stuff for the backpacker. Even today I still wonder if Paul didn't write the book with backpackers in mind. Of course, no legitimate commentary or theologian will admit it, but Paul must have been a backpacker.

We drove north about four hours to where we would start the trip. We were in the vicinity of Mount Shasta, but we would head toward a place called Glass Lake. It had been a favorite trek in the past, and we decided to make it again.

After the first day's hike, everything seemed to be perfect. The weather, the trail markers, our spirits—absolutely everything seemed to fare well. Although we traveled only about five miles, that was a good warm-up, considering the inexperience of the group.

That night, huddled around a warm fire, I read from Philippians 4:4-6: "Rejoice in the Lord always. I will say it again: Rejoice! . . . Do not be anxious about anything, but in everything, by prayer and petition, with thanksgiving, present your requests to God." Then I added, "Many of you are backpacking for the first time and feel some anxiety. Some are tired already. Some have blisters already. But let's rejoice in the Lord."

And we did. We sang songs a cappella, such as "She'll Be Comin'

Round the Mountain." But we finished with great gospel songs, such "The Blood Will Never Lose Its Power," and "Jesus Is the Answer."

I turned to Pastor Mike and asked, "Do you want to add anything?"

"No. You managed to say it all."

The next day was the most difficult hike of the entire trip. We wanted to get to Glass Lake, but we had nearly 15 miles to walk. Now, that doesn't sound like much, but try doing so with 50 pounds on your back. Plus, most of the trek was up a long stretch of switchbacks, until the last two miles that descended steeply into the small valley that cradled Glass Lake.

The switchbacks were narrow, and the footing was loose. A new girl in our group named Krystal stepped on a slick rock, and her ankle rolled in an awkward way. Bringing up the rear, I saw her collapse beneath her pack. The initial sound that escaped her mouth made me wonder if our trip was finished before hardly beginning. Pastor Mike inspected the ankle, then looked at me. "It's not broken, but it's badly sprained."

"I know I can make it if I can just get to Glass Lake," Krystal pleaded.

Pastor Mike closed his eyes for a few seconds to gather his thoughts, then he stood and said, "OK, group, let's see if we can redistribute Krystal's pack into our packs. If she walks without a pack and someone helps her, she can make it."

Unloading her food and clothes, we stuffed what we could into our own backpacks while Pastor Mike strapped her pack and its remaining contents onto his. He also had an ACE bandage in his pack, and he bound her ankle snugly.

Looking at how Pastor Mike now had two packs to carry, I asked, "Are you going to be OK with that?"

He had a strained look on his face, but he said, "Yep. I can make it."

We found a stick that helped Krystal walk, then most of the group—including me—went on ahead to set up camp, while Pastor Mike and two others stayed with her as she hobbled up the switchbacks and down to the lake.

When the sun had set but the sky was still light, we heard voices. It was Pastor Mike, Krystal, and the others. They were singing "Rejoice in the Lord always, and again I say rejoice." We cheered them as they entered the camp, already set up with a blazing fire.

That night Krystal's foot resembled an elephant's hoof, but she had good spirits. "Pastor Mike reminded me," she commented, "of a text that helped me—I don't know where it's found—that says 'I can do all things through Christ.'"

Glancing at Pastor Mike, I said, "Would you believe that that's my worship talk for tonight? I was going to read from Philippians 4:13: 'I can do all things through him who gives me strength.'"

Everyone was impressed. One even said, "That's too weird." Pastor Mike only smiled. I just said, "Didn't I tell you that Philippians was the backpacker's book?"

After more singing and discussion, I asked Pastor Mike, "So, you want to say anything?"

He answered matter-of-factly, "No, not really."

For the first time, I felt a bit annoyed. *He's getting paid to do this and I'm not,* I thought to myself. *So why am I doing all the work?* I felt emotionally and physically drained—and in some ways *spiritually* drained as well. In part because I felt tremendous pressure to ensure the trip's success, and in part because I felt as if I was doing more "giving" spiritually then I was "getting."

We had planned to stay at Glass Lake for a couple days, which was good for Krystal's throbbing elephant hoof.

Nearly every day Pastor Mike would take me aside and encourage me. He had such good things to say, and I absorbed them. Also, even though I happily plagiarized his comments for my evening worship talks, he never seemed to mind. I just couldn't figure out why he didn't say them himself.

On the last night of our trip, when our blisters were many and our granola bars were few, I offered a final worship talk. "Tomorrow's our last hike," I told them. "It's a hard one, but the end will be so worth it that you will forget all the hardship it took to get there." I read from Philippians 3:13, 14: "Forgetting what is behind and straining toward what is ahead, I press on toward the goal to win the prize for which God has called me heavenward in Christ Jesus." Then I said, "This may seem corny, but let's use tomorrow's hike—sore feet and all—as a metaphor for life's path. When we get to the end, let's see if we feel a hint of what Paul talks about here—about forgetting what is behind. The exhilaration we'll feel at the end of the trail will be a mere sliver of what we will feel one day when Jesus returns. Every hardship, every unexplained 'why' will seem irrelevant when we reach 'the prize.' But let's not forget to 'rejoice in the

Lord always,' otherwise we'll miss the joy of the trail itself."

I felt as if my mini sermon was clichéd and needed some profound words to back it up, so before we finished and went to bed, I asked Pastor Mike if he had any concluding remarks. He said no.

I doubt he could tell, but I felt frustrated, surprised, and a bit betrayed. I had never in my life met a pastor who would turn down an obvious opportunity to speak. Yet here Pastor Mike had spurned numerous opportunities. I appreciated his confidence in me, but what about pastoral authority? What about a pastor's prerogative to have the final say-so? Apparently Pastor Mike had never learned those things.

The next day was chilly. It was the first cold spell we'd had, and it couldn't have been a worse day for it. The last leg was only about six miles, but it was a brutal six miles, and the wind was in our faces. Krystal's foot was well enough so that she could handle her own pack, but hardly a one of us didn't have at least one nasty blister. My thighs and calves protested every step along the trail.

For the first time our group seemed to become exasperated. "Are we there yet?" was the perpetual gripe. Pastor Mike, however, seemed to be having the time of his life. He was nimble still, and he cheerfully urged us on. "Remember that text Mike read about pressing toward the goal. Keep pressing, gang!"

He isn't very preachy, I thought to myself, *but at least he's a good listener and a good motivator.*

When we reached the trail's end, we could see our church bus. The old school bus/yellow tank never looked so beautiful in our lives. It was only midafternoon, so Pastor Mike asked, "Hey, how about pizza?"

After a week of ramen, granola bars, and trail mix, pizza tasted like heavenly manna—except that manna was supposed to spoil overnight, and pizza only gets better. I remember sitting at the table in the pizzeria feeling exhausted. Physically drained, emotions shot, I had nothing left to give. But the truth was that nothing that had occurred on the trip seemed to bother me, because we were home free and eating pizza.

Pastor Mike sat by me and reached for a stringy slice of pineapple-and-cheese pizza. "Mike, you did a great job, and I bet you're exhausted."

"Yeah, I feel exhausted in about every way possible."

"What do you mean?"

"I wanted this experience to be memorable for everyone. I wanted everyone to have fun, to gain memories, and to get something spiritual. Right now I just feel as if I have nothing left to give."

"Welcome to the wonderful world of the youth pastor."

Then I turned to him and said, "But why didn't you say anything when I asked if you wanted to say something?"

"To be honest, it was hard to keep my mouth shut. But somehow I knew you were the right person to speak to these kids. And my job was to make sure you had something to give in the end."

"Being a youth pastor seems too much like work," I said. "It's rewarding enough, I'm sure, but excruciatingly hard work."

"Yes," he said, reflectively. "The way you felt about this backpack trip—wanting everyone to learn and to grow and to have a good time—is how youth pastors feel nearly every day."

I didn't have a response to that. Instead I just mouthed the word "Wow."

"Yep, only those who are called to feel as drained as you do right now should take the job."

Right then and there I decided that I wasn't equipped to take on that much stress, so I never became a youth pastor. But that hasn't kept me from becoming a one-person committee for the worldwide appreciation of youth pastors.

14

Why Is There a Nominating Committee to Nominate the Nominating Committee?

OUR CONGREGATION LOVED COMMITTEES, as so many do, and it seems as if we had one for everything. Of course there was the church board, but that was only the beginning of our plethora of such bodies. For example, we had a luncheon committee, at which I assume they planned church luncheons rather than merely enjoying them. I was always a little suspicious of the luncheon committee, however, because I knew that at least two of the members were partial to gelatin with carrot shavings—a definite red flag in my book.

We also had a health committee that worked autonomously from the luncheon committee, but I always imagined the two groups meeting in some dark alley to rumble like in *West Side Story*. (I can just see them pulling out switchblades and fighting over whether potlucks should allow participants to have a third helping or not.)

The church had a worship committee that did little worshiping but a whole lot of *talking* about worship. In addition, we had a landscape committee that never pulled a weed but sure griped about the azaleas. The public relations committee did little relating to the public, but they knew how to argue about the appropriate size for a concert poster on the bulletin board in the narthex. (The fruit of that committee's labor was a 16-page booklet that said—if I may condense their committee-ese—"a poster may be no larger than 11" by 17".)

I've never liked being on committees, which may disqualify me to write this chapter. But I'm married to a committeeholic, so I can appreciate those who enjoy a heaping helping of *Robert's Rules of Order*. And while

I may sound anti-bureaucracy (which I am), bear with me, as I intend to do the unthinkable and defend the long-maligned committee. Whether I'm persuasive or not will be a matter of opinion.

Even today I can recall vividly the first committee I ever served on, and I remember feeling flattered at being asked. Its very name sounded so indispensable: "The nominating committee to nominate the nominating committee."

The mandate of the committee seemed simple enough: Choose people who could ably choose people who could ably hold various church posts whose names would then be brought to a vote before the congregation as a whole. The entire thing seemed so deliciously bureaucratic.

Although I was the youngest voice on the committee, I was smart enough to recognize that I was a token member. After all, I was only about 15 and had very little to contribute. They said they were interested in having the voice of the youth heard on more committees, so it was a kind of age-based affirmative action. Still, I felt that maybe I could speak for my peers, and I took the role seriously.

After being invited to participate, I eagerly waited for the committee to meet. However, nearly a month passed, and I still hadn't heard from the chair—a large but soft-spoken man who had recently retired from the police force. I knew him as Mr. Jack, but everyone else called him Jackie. I never understood why they referred to him as Jackie, which sounded too feminine for a burly man who could easily slam a thug onto the pavement and cuff him if necessary.

At first I thought something might be wrong. Perhaps the church had disbanded the committee—or worse, had removed me from it. Later in life I realized that committees by design move slowly. They form slowly, they meet slowly, they discuss the minutes slowly, they tinker with the minutes slowly, they vote on the minutes slowly, they address new business slowly, and if they accomplish anything at all, they do it slowly. Finally, after weeks of anticipation, Mr. Jack called me with the date, time, and place for the upcoming committee. He spoke slowly, which is probably how he came to be the chair of the committee.

It consisted of five of us, and Mr. Jack outlined our goal as a group—to nominate five people who could form another committee. Not aware that simple solutions are so uncommitteelike, I wanted to shout, "Look around you. Here are five competent people who could do the job just fine. Let's nominate ourselves, and we can begin filling church posts immediately."

Oh, how naive I was. I was shameless.

Our committee pulled out the church directory—one of those glossy photo directories—that helped us place a face to names we didn't recognize. Someone would bring up a name, and the group would bat it around. But invariably a committee member found a reason to nix the nomination. "She's in the middle of a divorce, bless her heart"; "He serves every year"; "She's too new to the congregation"; "He doesn't pay enough tithe—or at least he certainly doesn't pay it to the church."

At first I sat in awe of the group, and I paid close attention to what seemed like a private flogging of our congregation—though fortunately, few knew what was happening to them. Skeletons flew out of closets so fast that one almost had to duck to avoid getting smacked by a femur.

I should note that no one on that committee could be described as "malicious," though my description of them seems negative. Furthermore, no one meant any harm to his or her fellow members. Rather, everyone felt a pressing drive to "do the right thing," which made the committee overly cautious and, subsequently and perhaps inevitably, overly critical.

I knew little about the "seedy" lives of our congregation, so the entire session was shocking and disappointing. But after listening, I got the hang of it and started suggesting a few gossipy reservations of my own. While a love for their church's machinery drove the others, I was simply enjoying my newfound power to affect people's fates.

Suddenly a terrifying idea struck me—with so many positions to fill in the church, how would the nominating committee, whom we were nominating, ever find enough good people to put into them. To listen to this group—including me—one would have concluded that no one was worthy to serve in the church. Considering my own personal skeletons, I doubted my own worthiness to serve on this committee.

After two hours of deliberation we had come up with a few prospects, but were unable to vote on any. As a result we agreed to meet once more—same time next week. Of course, we had to vote on the time and location of our next meeting, which required more deliberation than I ever dreamed necessary.

My dad, who's even more wary of committees than I am, asked, "So how was the famous nominating committee to nominate the nominating committee?"

"Well, we talked a lot, but got nothing done," I said. As drained as I felt, I figured we must have accomplished something, but I scratched my head and could think of nothing. "We did manage to set a time for the next meeting," I concluded.

"Yes, that seems to be the one thing committees are good at," my dad sighed, with an obvious air of experience.

At church that weekend I admit that I couldn't pay attention to anything that transpired on the platform. Instead I scanned the sanctuary and saw people whom I suddenly knew too much about. Even some I had long held in high regard seemed to shrink before my very eyes. When I agreed to join the nominating committee to nominate the nominating committee, I figured I was joining an elite but innocuous circle. Now I wasn't so sure it was so innocuous anymore.

We met the next week, and I was ready to establish our nominations and be done with it. The entire experience had left me jaded, and I preferred my naïveté. Fleetingly I wondered if I could somehow get it back, but naïveté is like air in a balloon—once the balloon has popped, there's no chance of ever retrieving that air again.

It was obvious that the other members on the committee were just as frustrated at having to meet a second time. The committee's chair, in his characteristically low-key manner, said, "All right, gang, let's get this done here and now." He sounded like a late-night TV cop, and we all focused our attention on the task at hand.

Once more we plowed our way through the directory, but seemed to hit the same snags again and again. One person was deemed too aggressive, another too passive, another too radical, another too conservative. Sometimes we'd agree on an individual but know that he or she would most likely decline the nomination if asked.

By now I began to feel an anxiety that ran deeply into my thighs. I call this strain of anxiety "the wiggles," because it sends my legs into mini-convulsions when I'm locked in a bad situation from which there seems to be no escape. I've never believed in the stereotypical hell—that flame-infested dungeon with little demons wielding pitchforks. However, if Dante, in his fourteenth-century epic *The Divine Comedy*, had wanted to write about a more terrifying "Inferno," he might have assigned his unfortunate sinners to bad committees rather than to descending spirals of fire. At least the fire seems to accomplish something.

After two hours of quibbling, we'd gotten nowhere. None of us could bear the thought of meeting again. Besides, the pastor was expecting a list of names that night, and we didn't want to disappoint him.

One of the least-outspoken members of our committee, a retired teacher whose middle name is "practical," said, "Why don't we simply nominate last year's nominating committee? They did a pretty good job, so let's nominate them again."

Ecstatic at her suggestion, we nearly leaped out of our chairs and onto the table. It was as if we were Columbus's crew just after someone had shouted, "Land ho!" We patted each other on the back and laughed out loud. Then there was a motion, a call for discussion (of which, fortunately, there was none), and a vote. After a closing prayer we happily went home.

It wasn't until I was in bed that I realized how we had proved ourselves to be a truly competent committee: We had managed to take a simple task and turn it into an arduous and acidic ordeal, only to arrive at an obvious resolution that anyone but a committee member could see.

I'd like to say that my first taste of committee work was an extreme and poor example. However, I've served on many, many church committees since, and I've discovered that my first experience was quite typical. Too often the committees have been so eager to jump through the manifold hoops that few cared to think about the implications of their decisions. Cynics often refer to such committees as "rubber stamps." On the other hand, I've been on a few committees in which individuals—including me—have focused on ridiculous minutia to the point where we accomplished nothing practical.

Am I being too blunt about church committees?

Probably. And too critical, as well. But I'm convinced we can solve the problem of church bureaucracy quite simply. We need only to assign the problem to a committee that will hammer out a proposal, then make recommendations to a larger committee that will make a final resolution to be brought to the congregation at large. At that point the congregation will vote on it, and *voilà!* the problem is solved.

Or maybe not.

Truth be told, I don't have an answer to bureaucracy. If I did, I'd win a Nobel Prize for sure. Not only would I have removed an annoying monkey wrench from the church's otherwise well-oiled machine, but I would also have solved the national debt and have removed the millstone from the neck of the world's economies. I'm sure the answer is out there, probably tied up in a committee somewhere.

Nor am I aware of any biblical wisdom that directly confronts the deep question: Why is there a nominating committee to nominate the nominating committee? Granted, the world has lots of more urgent questions, but I doubt that I'm the only one who has pondered that particular one. To be honest, when it comes time to nominate members of the nominating committee to nominate the nominating committee, there are usually more than a few chuckles. Apparently the reason for such a committee—in spite of obvious good intentions—is that that's the way it has always been done. And maybe that's reason enough.

To be honest, I kind of wish there really existed a "thus saith the Lord" that said, "No more nominating committees to nominate the nominating committees," or "If you must form committees, make sure they're quick and to the point." Alas, while the Bible writers had enormous foresight, they didn't have that kind of wisdom. (I'm sure they had better things to contemplate than ecclesiastical bureaucracy.)

Once when I bemoaned to a friend the lack of biblical guidance on the subject, he replied, "How about the passage that says, 'Everything should be done in a fitting and orderly way.'" The text he was referring to is 1 Corinthians 14:40, and only a good committee person such as my friend would cite such a passage in defense of committees.

"Nice try, Mr. Chairman," I told him, "but I think that passage is talking about how our worship should be orderly and never chaotic."

"OK," he countered, "but doesn't it say something about God not being a God of disorder?"

I looked it up, and what it really says is "God is not a God of disorder but of peace" (1 Corinthians 14:33). "Well, the disorder part fits," I commented, "but no one can tell me that 'peace' has anything to do with committees—at least very few of the ones I've served on."

But perhaps the most astounding aspect of this discussion is the manner in which I intend to switch sides and defend the seemingly indefensible. Though I loathe committees, and bureaucracy in general, I have come to believe they do have a place in the church. (If you only knew how difficult it is even to write such words, you would have enormous sympathy for me.)

I came to this apparent shift when considering Peter's radical statement: "But you are a chosen people, a royal priesthood, a holy nation, a people belonging to God, that you may declare the praises of him who called you out of darkness into his wonderful light" (1 Peter 2:9). Theologians have long interpreted this passage as a call for the "democratization of the gospel," meaning that individuals can approach God and his Holy Word directly, without being dependent on a priestly class. It seems like good theology, and I'm glad for it. God allows us enormous freedom to come to Him as an individual, and our pastors are not our intercessors or our lords, but rather more like peer guides. And yet, how is a church supposed to function smoothly when everyone is, in a spiritual sense, a "royal priest"? Though each of us may belong to a "holy priesthood," not everyone agrees on what to serve at the church picnic. What's more, some problems are too complex to solve with a simple democratic vote. Hence committees came into existence.

My point is not to endorse church bureaucracy, though God certainly did allow for certain categories within the church. He assigned roles to us, and "it was he who gave some to be apostles, some to be prophets, some to be evangelists, and some to be pastors and teachers, to prepare God's people for works of service, so that the body of Christ may be built up" (Ephesians 4:11, 12). Of course, Jesus is the head of the body, and we are connected to him, "held together by every supporting ligament" so that the church might grow "in love, as each part does its work" (verse 16).

Call this a stretch, but if the body of Christ is to function as a single body, it must have order. For there to be order, there must be individual parts—that is, body parts—working in unison with the others. But sometimes parts don't agree. Sometimes parts need the input of the other members. And sometimes multiple parts must join together to form a working structure—such as the body's cardiovascular or nervous systems.

Perhaps that's the best explanation for the inevitable bureaucracy in the church. The only thing that makes our human systems—à la committees—function a bit rougher than a bodily system—à la a cardiovascular system—is that we humans are stubborn, obtuse, independent, power-grabbing, free-thinking, and flawed. In short, we're human.

Despite our foreseeable foibles that seem to gum up the works sometimes, I'm glad that I belong to a church that values the opinions of its members and seeks those perspectives by means of, well, committees. I don't like it when committee members are rubber stamps, making the committee itself fruitless, but even in those situations the committee at least solicited opinions. Nor do I like it when Christian committee members forget Jesus' eleventh commandment given at the upper room—to love as He has loved us. Furthermore, I hope that church committees remember that God is the head of the body, and the committee is just a bodily system. (If the cardiovascular system starts to think it's the brain, we're all in trouble.) Though our systems are imperfect, they do have the benefit of preventing our congregations from becoming little fiefdoms ruled by the few.

OK, so I haven't answered the question "Why is there a nominating committee to nominate the nominating committee?" I'm not sure I've even adequately dealt with the issue of why there exists so much bureaucracy in the church. Maybe I'm ducking the question altogether because we haven't found a better way than our current system. God gave us tremendous guidelines and principles to help make an effective church body, but He bravely left most of the details to us. It's not in God's nature to send a sign from heaven or a "thus saith the Lord" when it comes to the minor stuff, such as what to serve at the next church social or who will be on the nominating committee.

I think it says a great deal about God that He allows us as a body the freedom to make our own choices—even if we do so in as convoluted a way as possible. And I think it says a great deal about us if the process of decision-making—i.e., committees—reflects the same love that God has for us.

Am I the Only Weird One Here?

AT TIMES I LOOK at my brothers and sisters in Christ—a.k.a. the church—and I wonder if I'm the only weird one around. Everyone seems pretty normal, at least more normal than I am.

I used to feel depressed about my strangeness, because I have more quirks and glitches than a beta version of Microsoft software. For example, I'd rather wear jeans and a luau shirt to church than a suit and tie, so I usually do. And, as I mentioned already, I'd rather hear a hymn done well than a praise song done poorly—and vice versa. I get an ache in my left molar when the church's piano slips out of tune. Also, I've considered conducting a scientific study to see just how long new pew smell lasts. Other times I have wondered when a pastor's weekend begins and ends. And what do pastors wear under their baptismal robes?

As you can see, I'm weird. It's not that I'm a bad guy, as such—I just think differently. Need more evidence?

Sometimes, when there is a bird or a chipmunk visible outside the window at church, I lose track of what the preacher is saying.

Often as I sit in church and watch that handsome couple walk down the aisle with their perfect children in their neatly ironed clothes, I try to imagine what their morning was like, which leads me to wonder whether they had as much trouble arriving at church on time as I did.

When old Mr. Joe gets up to welcome the visitors and says, "Isn't this a beautiful day?" as he always does, I wonder if he really means it. Maybe he burned his toast, as I did.

When the congregation and the organ get off sync with each other, I want to scream and run to the platform and count out time by stomping my foot and clapping my hands.

Even as a grown adult I have been known to reflect light onto the church's ceiling with my watch, maneuvering that reflection around an obstacle course of lighting fixtures, water stains, and rafters. (Michelle always punches me when she catches me doing this, so I don't recommend this activity to anyone with a sensitive arm.)

When I've listened to a soloist sing to a soundtrack, I've asked myself, "How many wars has our church sound system been through?" And why, after we purchased a $5,000 amplifier and a $15,000 set of speakers, is the microphone still not turned on?

During Communion, when the tiny wafers of unleavened bread have been passed in front of me, I've actually thought about scooping out a fistful for myself. (One wafer's not enough to tide me over until potluck.)

I actually like the old Disney movies they used to show at the church, and I wish they'd bring them back. Nothing makes me more nostalgic for the church's social life than classics such as *Pollyanna* or *The Snowball Express*. I even miss the restroom breaks while the projector guy changed the reels. (See? I *am* weird!)

I still think *Mission Spotlight* is exhilarating, more so than anything on the Travel Channel. I've even been tempted to shout "Encore!" when an episode ends.

When packing a "goody bag" to help keep Ramsey quiet during church, I like to include toys that will be fun for Dad, too. (Whoever said Legos were for kids alone?)

The bottom line is that I'm a bit weird. There's no one quite like me, and let's hope—for the sake of the world's sanity—there never will be. And even though I have felt many times like an island of weirdness adrift in a sea of normalcy, I know that I'm not the only offbeat one in the church. But sometimes I have to take that knowledge on faith alone.

A very close pastor friend of mine used to say, "God never loves us because of who we are—He loves us in spite of who we are." I think he's right. If given a chance to see the real me, most people would be somewhat repulsed. I don't say that because I'm an especially loathsome person, but rather because I'm a human being. When the Bible says in Romans 3:23 that "all have sinned and fall short of the glory of God," it means that we're all a bit messed up. And yet, in spite of ourselves, "God so loved the world that he gave his one and only son" (John 3:16).

Now that I think about it, perhaps my friend's assessment is not entirely right. It's not so much that God loves us *in spite* of who we are, it's more that He loves us *because of who He is*.

But not all of my weirdness is a product of sin. Nor is it all accidental. A great deal of it is a product of God's intentional creativity. Yes, when the Creator made me, He must have been in a funny mood. Psalm 139:13, 14 says: "You created my inmost being; you knit me together in my mother's womb. I praise you because I am fearfully and wonderfully made; your works are wonderful." Apparently God had some say into how I turned out, and from the day I was born, practically, I've been a little weird. I used to be a little embarrassed about that, but now I'm OK with it. I'm OK with it, first of all, because God must have had a need for a weird guy in the world, otherwise He wouldn't have made me. And second, I'm just one of 6 billion other weird people in the world. That should make me feel less weird, but fortunately it only makes me more conscious of my weirdness.

The problem is, I wasn't always OK with being weird. I wanted desperately to be normal, or at least to appear normal.

I attended a boarding high school, Rio Lindo Academy, for my junior and senior years. The advantage to boarding school—or at least the one I attended—is that the quality of education is high and the potential to get into big trouble is usually low. That's because one never escapes the Big Brother eyes of the school's faculty and staff. I enjoyed the experience immensely and am currently the president of Rio Lindo's alumni association. However, one aspect of boarding school drained me until I was sick: I couldn't easily hide the real me.

It's easy to wear a mask when you can go home at the end of each day. But in a boarding school students live close together in tiny stalls called dormitory rooms. If you are angry, moody, or aloof, somebody is bound to see it, and the mask gets stripped away. And I didn't like that.

I've always been the type who keeps my emotions to myself. Sure, the weird wheels in my head were well oiled, but I just didn't want anyone peeking inside to see them turning. I'm so private that I find it stressful shopping for CDs in a music store because my selections may reveal too much about myself. OK, so I probably need therapy, but that's off the subject. The point is, I spent two years endeavoring to keep even my two roommates from observing too much of me.

I must have been at least partially successful. Not long ago I was browsing through my old school yearbook, laughing at the photos. (We thought we were so hip back then with our mid-1980s argyle sweaters and parachute pants. It was the era when, as Huey Lewis sang, it was "hip to be square." As I perused the yearbook, the various notes from classmates intrigued me the most. They were fond messages from friends I vowed I'd never forget, and yet now many seemed completely unknown to me.

One friend whom I worked with in the Career Center for two years wrote, "Mike, you're a great guy. I just wish I could have gotten to know you better. You're a hard person to know."

I remember reading that inscription 17 years ago and being proud of it. It proved that I had maneuvered through two years of campus life without revealing who I really was. As I read it now, however, I feel sad, because I've come to terms with myself. I recognize that I'm a bit weird, and I'm OK with it. Frequently I don't always see the world—or the church—as others do, and again I'm OK with that. And I realize that I can't control whether or not people like me.

So am I the only weird one in the church? Fortunately, no. I'm one of many, many, many. I'm sure there are a few normal ones out there, those theoretical individuals who have never asked such pointed questions as "Sometimes church is boring—is that OK?" Or "Why do some potluck entrées scare me?" Or "What is the pastor wearing under that baptismal robe?"

Long ago as a little boy I asked my mom if she thought I would ever get married. She said, "Oh, God has someone in mind for you. But she'll have to be a little weird, because it takes a weird one to love a weird one."

I was satisfied by that answer. And sure enough, she proved almost prophetic: I married a wonderful woman who's nearly (but not quite) as weird as I am. (Michelle will appreciate that line, no doubt!) That's because it takes a weird one to love a weird one. And similarly, because God loves me, He must have a special place in His heart—a wonderfully weird place—for weird ones.